THE DISCIPLINE OF NATURE:

ARCHITECT ALFRED BROWNING PARKER IN FLORIDA

September 24, 2016 – February 26, 2017

Organized by HISTORY**MIAMI** MUSEUM

Allan T. Shulman and Randolph C. Henning, Guest Curators

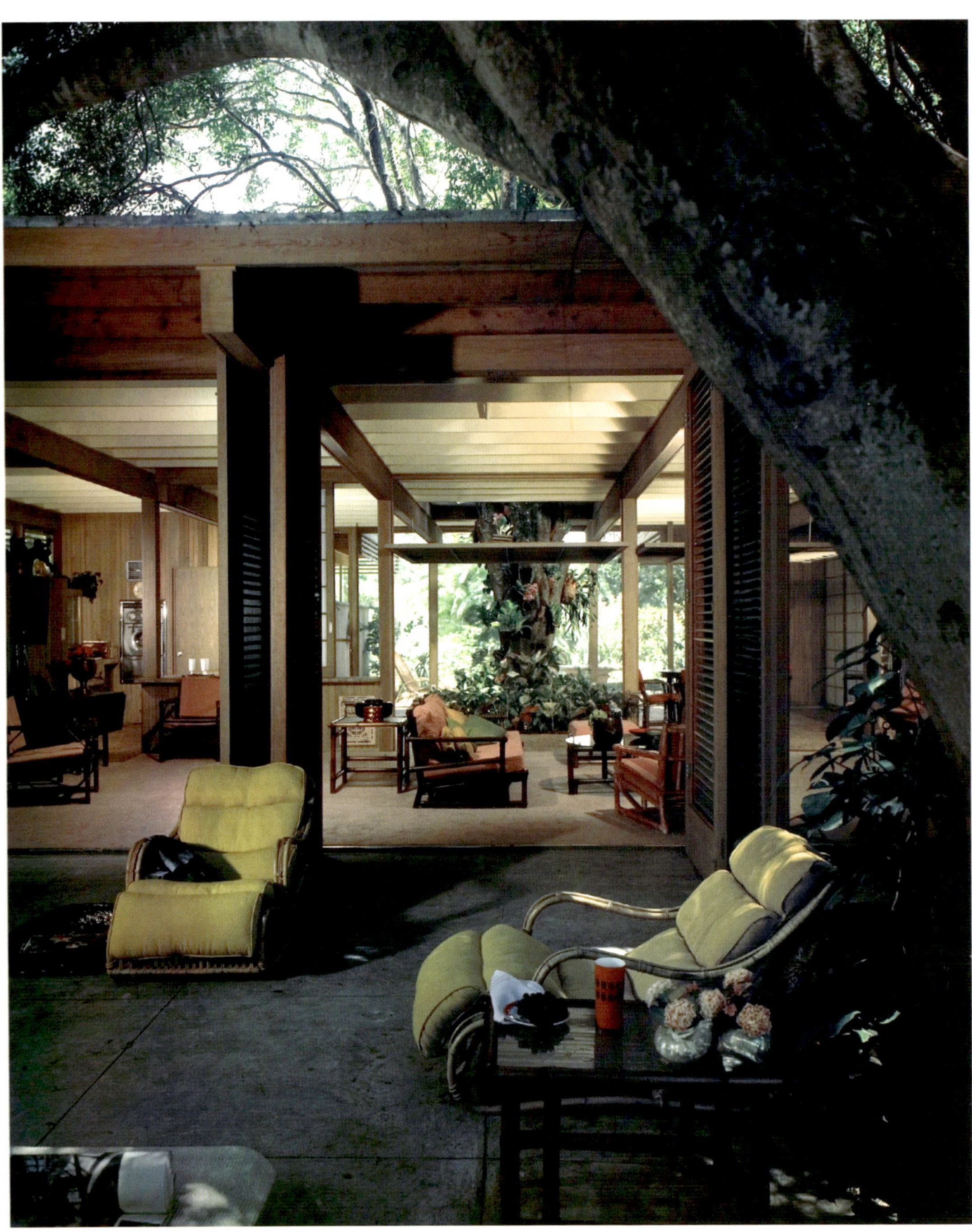

President's Message

HistoryMiami Museum is proud to celebrate the 100th anniversary of Alfred Browning Parker's birth with *The Discipline of Nature: Architect Alfred Browning Parker in Florida.* As an institution dedicated to telling Miami's stories, it's our pleasure to feature this exhibition highlighting the Florida work that made Parker an architectural icon in Miami and beyond.

I would like to thank our guest curators, Allan T. Shulman and Randolph C. Henning, who contributed their keen insight into Parker's life and career. It has been a truly rewarding experience for our staff to work with them and to make Parker's work accessible to a wide audience. They have a true passion and tireless enthusiasm for his legacy. Finally, we couldn't have developed this exhibition without the hard work of the dedicated museum Board of Trustees and my good colleagues.

The Museum is a destination for visitors from around the world and an invaluable resource for the South Florida community. Our collections include the Woodrow W. Wilkins Archives of Architectural Records, which were formed in 1982 in honor of Woody Wilkins, a former professor at the University of Miami's School of Architecture and Museum trustee. The archives include drawings, photographic material, office and project files, models, and architectural fragments pertaining to noteworthy individual buildings and to prominent architects and architectural firms ranging from the Mediterranean Revival work of Walter DeGarmo to the Modernism of Igor Polevitzky to the Postmodernism of Arquitectonica. The architectural collections are supported by other materials in our archives, particularly our photographic holdings. We house nearly 1.5 million images dating back to the 1880s.

Through our collections, exhibitions, and programs we strive to connect people by telling the stories of Miami's communities, individuals, places, and events. We hope you will come explore the past in hopes of inspiring the future.

Stuart A. Chase
President/CEO, HistoryMiami Museum

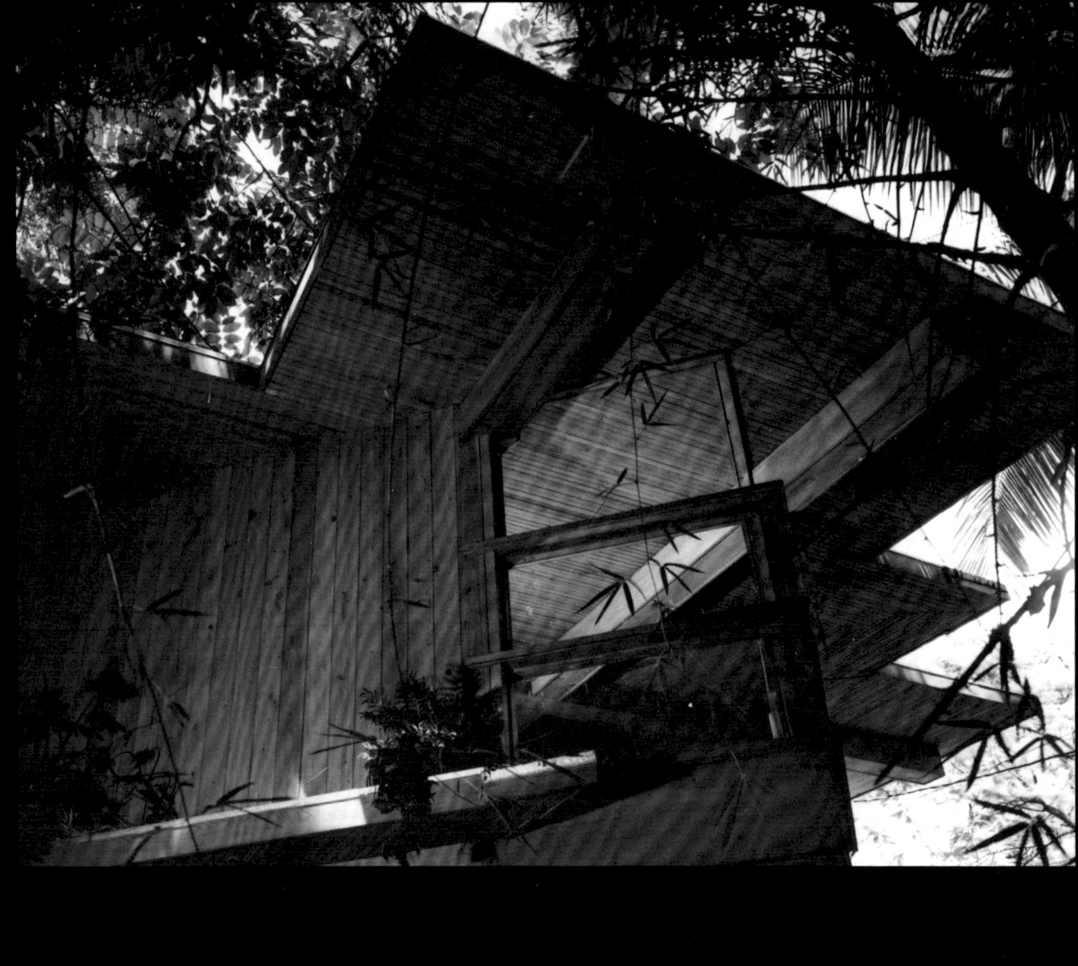

The Discipline of Nature: Architect Alfred Browning Parker in Florida

Allan T. Shulman

Among the modernist architects who transformed postwar Florida into a laboratory of regionalist architecture, Alfred Browning Parker was an iconoclast. He shared the conviction, common among young architects in Miami, that an authentic regional architecture had not yet been 'invented.'[1] Inspired by the power of place and eager to innovate, Parker became a disciple of American traditions and the region's foremost organic architect.

Extrapolating from Frank Lloyd Wright's position on the architect's role in society, Parker believed that architecture could be a harbinger of an authentic regional culture in Miami. He developed an architectural syntax that emphasized the centrality of human endeavor, in which design integrity was transcendent. Parker's position derived from a deep respect for the earth and its resources, as well as a moral and aesthetic interest in the power of nature as a vital and rational force. He saw ecology as a guide to understanding resources and their interaction, and also as a discipline for ethical thinking capable of shaping an architectural response.

Yet he also held a romantic view of the natural world, at once inspiring architectural ornament and offering a metaphor for design integrity. Parker promoted such values as beauty, craftsmanship, fitness, appropriateness, utility, unity, and balance. He subscribed to what theologian and philosopher Albert Schweitzer called "reverence for life,"[2] finding purpose in a spiritual relationship with the universe generally, and the ecology of the planet specifically. He noted, "We should judge architecture by how well it serves the growth of the human spirit."[3]

Throughout a career that stretched from 1942 until his death in 2011, Parker translated his ideals into tropicalist buildings that shaped the suburban and urban landscapes of Florida. A builder, businessman, artist, sculptor, furniture-maker, and teacher, he was also one of the few Florida architects to lecture on and publish his ideas. He produced essays and eventually a book to document his theories.

Parker's organic Florida architecture made him a regional figure and a national icon. His collaboration with the influential *House Beautiful* editor Elizabeth Gordon situated his Miami work, particularly his interpretation of the single-family home, in the national debate about modern American architecture. Parker's expression of organic architecture changed over the course of his career, partly in response to national trends, but always in step with Florida's maturity. Through his iterative forms, types, and constructive patterns he confirmed that change is "a sure law of the universe."[4] In the search for equilibrium between perpetual change and heartfelt principles, Parker distinguished himself as an extraordinary innovator.

Part I: In search of a discipline (1935-1942)

God forbid that man, whose instructor is the whole of nature, should become a wax lump, in which a professor impresses his sublime image. – Georg Christoph Lichtenberg, as quoted by Alfred Browning Parker[5]

Alfred Browning Parker was born in 1916 in Boston, Massachusetts and raised in Miami. He attended the University of Florida's School of Architecture and Allied Arts from 1935 to 1939, where he studied with Rudolph Weaver, the School's founding director. Under Weaver, the curriculum emphasized the constructive arts and the fundamentals of architectural form and

Gayer Residence, Coconut Grove, 1953
Photograph © Ezra Stoller/ESTO
ESTO

beauty. Parker soon evinced an interest in practical, honest approaches to building, inspired by natural forms and processes and by the philosophy of the 19th century American naturalists.

Parker proved receptive both to the revolution of Modern architecture and to continuity with vernacular traditions. He embraced the influence of the Arts & Crafts movement and the organic school of American architecture, especially the three architects he called the 'traditionists:'[6] H. H. Richardson, Louis Sullivan, and Frank Lloyd Wright. Wright in particular held new relevance in American architecture in the 1930s, with the completion of Fallingwater (1934-37), the Johnson Wax Headquarters (1936-39), and Florida Southern College (beginning in 1938).[7] Parker was inspired by Wright's national and regional perspectives, which advocated a connection to natural principles like democracy and organic architecture.

After graduation, Parker traveled abroad. In 1939, he received a Scandinavian American Foundation Scholarship to study at the Royal Academy of Free Arts in Stockholm, and in 1940, he earned a Pan American Airways Traveling Fellowship for research in Mexico.[8] Far from home, the young architect observed patterns of land and human building in sketchbooks. His sketches show an interest in authentic paradigms of landscape and tradition, the tenets behind the complex working of the earth, and the search for universal principles.

Parker's early drawings depicted industrial landscapes, historic landmarks, and rural scenes populated with thatched-roofed houses and barns, offering a view of Sweden that curiously excluded Modernist works. In Mexico, Parker illustrated the stone construction of the ancients and Spanish colonial structures, as well as street scenes silhouetted against typical landscapes. He rendered classical building features, perhaps in order to better understand their ornament. By contrast, his sketches of modern buildings were drawn in pen, often with notations explaining principles of structure, material use, and climate adaptation. Parker also used a Leica camera to capture over 600 black-and-white photographs and 200 color slides, planning to exhibit these in the United States.[9]

Back in the US, Parker found employment in the offices of his former professor, Rudolph Weaver, and was appointed to the faculty of his alma mater. He read assiduously, acquiring books on architecture and urban planning, landscape and horticulture, ecology, philosophy, and natural sciences, as well as works of poetry and illustrated collections of verse and quotations.[10] Among his favorite works during this period were those of the American naturalists Ralph Waldo Emerson, Walt Whitman, Henry David Thoreau, and Oliver Wendell Holmes.[11]

Parker kept diaries during his early professional life, recording his impressions and sketches in Lefax binders. Here he mixed poetry and practical notes with musings on truth, beauty, love, and spirituality. In one entry, he noted: "This little space of time and earth is ours! This to live! This to Know! This now to have!"[12] In another, he wrote: "We are all architects of the land."[13]

In these reflections, Parker found the beginning of a paradigm for an architectural discipline derived from nature. Perhaps influenced by Wright, the diarist was drawn to the idea that architecture could be taught by natural principle.[14] He formulated his own ideas about organic architecture, characterized by such intrinsic values as sincerity and simplicity, strength and repose, and the search for universal form. Committed to an ethical model for architecture, in which all building resources (land, materials, design) have artistic and spiritual dimensions, Parker pondered the nature of harmony:

Many things are summed up in the word UNITY. Unity meaning oneness, wholeness, completeness, describes the desirable relation between the land and the building, the form and the function, the materials and their appropriate uses, and the proper adaptation of techniques to the materials. Harmony is a direct consequence of the above relations.[15]

Decades later, the architect would summarize his discipline of architecture in five simple maxims: "build strongly; build as directly as possible with no complications; use the materials at hand and keep these as few as you can; let your building love its site and glorify its climate; design for use – make it beautiful."[16]

Part II: Manifestos of self-sufficiency (1942-1951)

Of all the arts, the art of building is the most useful and valuable to man. It is necessarily so, for one of man's first requirements is a shelter… He perceives that every person alive, though half of them aren't aware of it themselves, desires to live with some dignity and artistry, with a comfortable margin of leisure to develop the mind and soul. – Alfred Browning Parker [17]

In March 1942, Parker entered the US Naval Reserve as an intelligence officer. His service brought him back to Miami, on the cusp of a new phase in the city's growth. Parker's early design proposals, many developed while he was still in the Navy, show that he was inspired by the needs of Miami's growing population and interested in how Modern architecture could be adapted to this subtropical region.

Seeking a meaningful relationship among climate, landscape, and architecture, Parker explored Florida's environment as ecology, influenced by the region's small but well-established community of naturalist writers, horticulturists, and botanists, most notably John C. Gifford.[18] A botanist and tropical forester, Gifford became the young architect's newest mentor and, after Parker married Martha Gifford in 1942, his father-in-law. Gifford wrote extensively about Florida's landscape and was the first Miamian to publish ideas about the tropical home.[19] The botanist's 1911 treatise on Florida houses asserted a scientific principle of adaptation translated to architecture and speculated that the built environment should evolve organically. Of particular note, Gifford defined a concept of ecology that embraced usefulness and beauty as part of nature. In his book *The Tropical Subsistence Homestead*, Gifford articulated Emersonian principles of regional self-reliance. He proposed the agricultural 'homestead' as the ideal basis for a well-rooted democratic society, suggesting that the Everglades frontier that stretched west from Miami be divided into five-acre plots to be claimed by productive labor.[20]

Gifford's subsistence homesteads were a blueprint for an idealized model of land organization with unexpected overtones from Frank Lloyd Wright's Broadacre City, the agrarian vision first presented in *The Disappearing City* in 1932. In 1942, Parker gave architectural form to Gifford's land proposals, merging them with what he called the architectural "essentials of Florida living – outdoor space protected from mosquitos, airiness, light, protection from tropical rains, big living spaces, coolness, and 'atmosphere.'"[21] Although never built, his proposal for a two-story homestead, with floors of native rock, built-in furniture, and an airy second floor living space anchored by its chimney, would strongly influence his later work.

In 1943, while still in the Navy, Parker designed and built, with his own hands, a home and office for his young family in Coconut Grove. Due to war-time restrictions, but also with a mindful air of asceticism, his miniature home was fashioned with salvaged materials upon the ruins of an old gas station. Parker extrapolated the structure's vernacular construction into a modern synthesis: the artful rusticity of exposed oolitic rock walls and wood beams hewn from the trunks of native pine contrasted with curtains of glass window wall at either end. The single room, designed following an open plan layout centered on the oolitic stone hearth, suggested a remarkably simple domesticity. For Parker, this approach to construction was not just an act of homeowner bricolage; rather, it merged natural and human resources in a manifesto of self-sufficiency.

Architect-Builder-Developer

Discharged from the Navy in 1946, Parker opened what he called a 'workshop for the practice of architecture.' His professional shingle, imprinted on a piece of driftwood, hung outside his home, now enlarged with a second-floor studio. Over the next several years, he merged his activities as architect with those of builder and developer, transforming the Gifford/Parker philosophy of self-sufficiency into his business model. His interests evolved toward simple, expandable home types, often designed for commercial builders working in Miami's rapidly swelling suburbs.

Though his office was located in Miami, Parker continued to teach at the University of Florida. In Gainesville, the architect developed a modest two-story home for his family that derived in part from his earlier Tropical Subsistence Homestead experiments. Built in 1946 in only six weeks, its sturdy ground floor was built of exposed concrete block in alternating tall and short courses, while the upper story was constructed of wood and clad in vertical siding painted green to merge with the landscape.

Back in Miami, Parker launched his office with the Hopwood (1948) and Chandler (1949) residences in Coconut Grove, designing and constructing two wood homes around a 'borrow pit,' or quarry. Such borrow pits were often considered a blight, but as A.D. Barnes, Miami's first Parks director, had demonstrated, they could be made beautiful. Indeed, Parker transformed the rock pit floors into sunken gardens, and constructed stairs and ramps connecting to the houses, which were cantilevered from the plinth of rock to enjoy the tradewinds and views. These early homes revealed a new vocabulary, fusing indigenous materials like oolitic rock with unfinished pine board and batten walls, mono-pitch roofs, projecting wood awning windows, tile floors, and grass mat carpets.

In 1949, in the pinelands of South Miami, Parker expanded this vocabulary further. At the home he called "Rocks and Short Pines," he scattered the elements of the house as a rambling assemblage of low-slung clerestoried pavilions joined with screened breezeways. The influence of Japanese domestic architecture was evident in the home, which combined enclosed verandas, raised living areas, sliding wood and glass doors, and an open corner supported on an undressed trunk of pine.

Tropical and minimalist

Parker revealed another face to his rustic minimalism with a one-room cabin design. This "Ur-dwelling," first introduced in resort projects like Thunderbird (1945) in Lake Santeetlah, North Carolina, achieved particular clarity as a model home designed to meet the needs of returning G.I.s: the Tropex-pansible Home (1948). Attempting to achieve extraordinary efficiency, Parker circumscribed all house functions into a simple volume, used an open plan layout, and extended the interior space into a screened porch.

The progressive unfolding of a tropical house into a screened enclosure was developed thematically at the linear Litsey Residence (1952), where the mass of stone and wood on one side of the house contrasted with an ethereal screened pool enclosure on the other. An essential dualism played across the section of the home. It was half buried, protected from the street by a low berm, and half exposed. A butterfly roof framed with bents of salvaged native pine joined the opposites, and the home was carefully structured as a series of square bays, demonstrating a new geometric rigor. Curving site walls of oolitic rock playfully projected in and out of this regular system.

The Litsey Residence was likely Parker's earliest use of mahogany *persianas*, a door system customarily found in the Caribbean and incorporating adjustable slats.[22] Used as a wall system built as architectural carpentry, persianas were essential to the aesthetic of Parker's early homes, and an example of their adaptation to Florida's climate. This single device controlled light, ventilation, glare, privacy, and views, allowing the house to function as an environmental machine.[23]

Although Parker's early career was largely defined by well-crafted custom homes, the architect also embraced the organizational models and construction techniques of the 'builder's home.' In 1940s South Florida, merchant housing was being delivered by the thousands of units to G.I.s and to the expanding middle class. Parker designed more than 1,500 such homes along the periphery of Miami, in places like the Essex Village Subdivision (1949) in Hialeah. He developed efficient open plans with flowing spaces, exposed roof framing, generous windows, broadly projecting eaves and gables, carports, and porches. Using a builder's material palette – concrete slab-on-grade, stuccoed masonry block walls, and a wood frame roof – Parker influenced the development of everyday suburban homes.

Parker also applied his environmental consciousness to schools. An early design for the Institute for Non-Aristotelian Research and Education (1944) in South Miami shows an awareness of the progressive school designs by Richard Neutra in Los Angeles and Vladimir Ossipoff in Hawaii,[24] as well as Wright's work at Florida Southern College. Parker applied similar progressive principles in his 1949 addition to George Washington Carver School in Coral Gables. Here, classrooms with exposed concrete structural joists opened to broad courtyards through 'light-directing panels' that reduced glare and maximized natural light and fresh air. Saw-tooth roofs covered the art studios, while the gymnasium was sheltered by a quonset-type parabolic roof built of tapered pre-cast concrete arched ribs and stressed skin panels.

Part III: Regional and Modern (1952-1961)

By mid-century, Parker had established a thriving practice in Miami. While house commissions boomed, he also designed small commercial buildings and the prestigious Bal Harbour Club. Parker advanced his brand of organic architecture by testing the boundaries between regional and modern design. He explored the structural capacities of concrete and steel and incorporated a more cultivated sensibility in his use of native materials. He also invented new types of indoor-outdoor connectivity, and used geometry in a more disciplined way, most notably in decorative systems that were closely integrated into his buildings.

These strategies appear prominently in a novel home he designed and built in 1952 for his family in Coconut Grove. Perched on a stone bluff overlooking Biscayne Bay, the Parker Residence was fashioned out of the very land on which it stood. Battered stone walls of native oolitic rock rose from the ridge, embedded with salvaged stone sculptures, painted tiles, and carved marble. These lithic ramparts framed a multilevel deck system of concrete plates that commanded open vistas of the bay through deeply recessed screens of mahogany persianas.[25] Above, a 'sky garden' and small rooftop retreat were nestled beneath the treetops. Warmth and a connection to nature were transmitted inside by terrazzo floors, cork ceilings, stone coursing, wood-paneled walls, and built-in wood furniture laced with open webbing, caning, or leather.

The residence also integrated architecture, furnishings, and art, a principle objective of organic design.[26] Parker embraced the idea of a decorative order, which was eschewed by many Modernists, but was a critical discourse in American architecture, spanning the transcendentalism of Louis Sullivan, the projective ornament of Claude Bragdon, and the geometric composition of Wright.[27] Parker based his decorative system on pure geometries, crystalline forms, mathematical patterns, and a search for harmony. He sculpted geometric motives into decorative friezes in concrete and stone, and employed a graphic abstraction of the house's floating planes as a leitmotif in fabric designs and in his own stationery. He also collaborated with textile artist Mariska Karasz to develop textile and carpet designs unique to the home, and stocked the rooms with carefully chosen modern furnishings.

Even before completion, the bayfront home attracted the attention of *House Beautiful* editor Elizabeth Gordon, who published the Parker Residence as the magazine's "Pace Setter 1954" – its prestigious yearly feature home. Few friends were as instrumental to Parker's success as Gordon: *House Beautiful* was a premier shelter magazine, and the editor introduced her readers to progressive American design. In featuring the home, Gordon promoted Parker's organic approach as a new type of modern American architecture, bringing the architect acclaim from coast-to-coast, including from his hero Wright, who endorsed the home as true organic architecture.

Parker pressed further with open systems of construction, made possible by the use of concrete and steel, in projects like the Bal Harbour Club (1952) and Mass Residence (1954) in Palm Beach. The club, for instance, was raised on concrete pylons over a flat waterfront site. Its free-plan interior layout, wrapping persiana doors, and shade-producing cantilevers exhibited a breezy openness; this was one way of idealizing a tropical structure.[28] A similar tray-like configuration was used at the Mass Residence, offering a cantilevered terrace toward the water. Raised over an oolitic stone plinth that cradled the main living area, the gabled form of the home resulted from its unusual 30-60-90 degree structural steel frames.

House type experiments

The rush of new commissions for exquisitely finished homes, unique to each site, eclipsed Parker's earlier interest in the home as a self-empowering system. Responding to the individual needs of each site and each family, Parker conducted countless experiments in organic architecture, expressing the diversity and typological variation of nature as a vital force shaping patterned architectural responses.

One house type, with roots in the wood vernacular traditions of Coconut Grove, comprised a small, wood-built pavilion, or assemblage of pavilions, where, Parker observed, "a single person who enjoys the simple pleasures may live and entertain."[29] Journalist and environmentalist Marjory Stoneman Douglas called these little structures "August Moon tea houses."[30] The Gayer Residence (1953), two square pavilions connected along a diagonal axis, introduced the type. The play of squares included rotations and intersections that activated both the exterior and interior volumes. Even the broadly cantilevered flat roof was rotated 45 degrees, and structured so that the corners of the main pavilion were cut away. Nearly all domestic elements, including shelves and seating, were built into lightweight wood walls; only the stone hearth stabilized the home.

In contrast, the compact Ewing Residence (1955) comprised only a single square pavilion, cantilevered over a smaller masonry base (reminiscent of Parker's earlier Tropical Subsistence Homestead). On the upper level, beneath the pyramidal roof, low walls, built-in furniture and a floating copper fireplace subtly divided the one-room space. A square 'tree verandah,' located beneath the canopy of a giant banyan tree, provided a remarkable outdoor analogue to the vaulted interior volume of the house. An exterior switchback ramp connected the garden, tree verandah and raised living area, celebrating movement between them.

The pavilion type reached critical definition at the Jewel Parker Residence (1957), designed for Parker's mother. Two square pavilions, one raised and the other on the ground, were dynamically arranged around a tiled patio. Pyramidal roofs and persiana doors made the pavilions lofty and expansive; the main pavilion comprised nearly three levels beneath its exposed roof. In this space, diverse functional elements were wrapped into compact, well-integrated packages around a central hearth-like core that in fact distributed cool air throughout the home. The post and beam construction echoed the great banyan tree, a remarkable symbiosis of architecture and environment in forested Coconut Grove. The pavilion type, however, was soon recast as a tropical 'island residence' in the homes Parker designed in Jamaica, the Bahamas, and the Leeward island of Isle St. Martin.[31]

In contrast to these delicate pavilions, Parker developed one-story houses that emphasized economy and the kinship of building to ground. Likely inspired by Wright's 1930s-era Usonian houses, these modest structures blended standardized wood and masonry elements to permit easy construction. They had narrow, 'in-line' plan configurations that allowed effective cross ventilation and a close integration of house and site.

The one-bedroom Friedman Residence (1953) in Coconut Grove exploited that integration with a gabled roof that extended the central living area into the home's front and back yards through persiana doors. The living area of the Marko Residence (1955) in Coconut Grove was similarly flanked by outdoor living areas. Cuban persianas and shoji-like Japanese paper screens signified a seamless integration of indoors and outdoors. The home's constructive integrity was also on display, with exposed wood columns and beams offset by the solidity of the hearth and the long masonry wall used to screen the street. Here, Parker used exposed concrete blocks as a decorative system, a low-cost alternative to both the 'textile blocks' used by Wright and the exposed oolitic rock of Parker's early homes.

The Kitchens Residence (1956) in unincorporated Miami-Dade County was similarly remarkable for its frank constructive logic and rustic materiality. Tidewater red cypress board and batten panels spanned between the masonry piers supporting its gabled roof trusses. In the piers, and in the prow-like hearth that occupied one narrow end of the house, exposed concrete blocks alternated with slump brick courses for visual effect. Parker also designed such in-line houses with hexagonal and even rhomboid grids. The latter was used at the Good Residence (1960) in Sea Ranch Lakes, producing a diamond-shaped living area that pivoted around the hearth. Exposed masonry block, terrazzo, and hand-woven carpets combined with plaster and cypress to provide both natural warmth and a graphic emphasis.

Parker's organic architecture extended to a fascination with tower forms and the potential of towers to command landscape from heights. The architect had already designed an observation tower to complement the Bazaar International Mall (1958) in Riviera Beach, a 230-foot concrete trylon formed in concrete and topped by a 60-foot tapered aluminum mast. Next he explored how the type could be translated into tropicalist home designs. Parker's first tower house proposal, for the Belin Residence (1959), was pagoda-like – comprising a single room per floor to promote positive cross-ventilation. The functional issues of such narrow structures were addressed by marrying its vertical form to a sprawling ground floor pedestal. The tower rose to four stories in a series of cantilevered concrete plates, using waffle slab construction to cantilever from columns in both directions. A structural core on the backside contained stairs, elevator, and bathroom. Persiana doors opened to terraces with planters that would have sent green cascading down the building. The Marathon Shores residence for conservationist Mary Crane (1972) was even taller: six floors, including the roof terrace. In this design, illustrative of Parker's later interest in bold forms, shingled side walls betrayed a greater sense of volume, and the home's living and dining rooms were located on the second and third floors, allowing the ground floor to be given over to indoor-outdoor spaces like a Florida Room and a slat house for orchids.

Another experiment in home architecture involved pod arrangements, in which the distinct programs of the site – living, dining, and sleeping – were scattered in separate structures (an approach that re-engaged Parker's earlier organizational experiment at Rocks and Short Pines). As was so often the case, the experiment, or mutation, began with the architect's own new home, Woodsong (1967). Located on a densely wooded site in Coconut Grove, the home was organized into three independent pods tethered to a sinuous outdoor pool and covered boardwalk, enabling residents to swim from room to room. Each pod had the simplicity and organizational rigor of Parker's one-room houses, employing split-level spatiality and double-height spaces. In contrast to the architect's earlier pavilion houses, each pod was a sculptural block whose continuous wood-slatted skin expressed pure volume and futuristic plasticity, as well as exposing the stalks of surrounding palms.[32]

Parker also proposed a house type that turned inward on itself. The Miller Residence (1957) in Coconut Grove was organized around a 40' by 40' atrium that offered a type of communal space rarely found in homes. All areas of the house, including the backyard, pivoted from this dominant, luminous space, delimited by cypress wood piers and crowned by a metallic space frame. Wright had made the atrium a central idea of his non-domestic work,[33] but Parker explored the type as a technique of suburban introversion. As *House Beautiful*, which featured the house as its Pace Setter 1959, explained, the home "offers its residents more control over their environment than has ever been known in America."[34]

The atrium provided a foil for new types of spatial complexity, including diagonal views, rotary circulation that circumnavigated the atrium, and living areas withdrawn under varying ceiling levels to emphasize a sense of spatial compression and release. The atrium, moreover, permitted the exposition of eye-catching structural experiments, from the powerful concrete arms used to support the screened atrium of the unbuilt Woronzow Residence (1959) in Coconut Grove, to the tent-like glue-laminated bents of the *Popular Mechanics* "Minimum Maintenance House" (1961) and Bieglesen Residence (1961) in Hollywood.

The powerful vaults of the atrium houses suggested a central role for space in planning, an idea Parker also found especially appropriate for houses of worship. In his religious works, he developed a syntax of tall arches that delimit space while suggesting vaults. For instance, at the House of God at Vista Memorial Gardens (1958) in Miami Lakes, Parker used a circle of concrete arches to enclose a grassy knoll and frame the open vault of the sky, a classical gesture that attests to the marking of place. Similarly, the wood-constructed Hope Lutheran Church (1962) in South Miami employed a series of glue-laminated vaulted arches, creating the communal space and skyward orientation of a traditional cathedral. As Parker noted, "The heart of the matter in architecture is the enclosure of space. As with individuals, the best part should be on the inside."[35] Over time, Parker's use of vaults migrated from traditional gestures toward organic practices. The Fread Sanctuary of Temple Beth El (1971) in West Palm Beach was inspired by the chambered shell of the marine mollusk, *Nautilus Pompilius*. The sanctuary's 24 glue-laminated arches of southern yellow pine spiraled at 15-degree intervals, and rose to a great clerestory window that bathed the Bima, or altar, in southern light.[36]

A philosophy

Through his work, Parker honed a philosophy that he elaborated in *You and Architecture: A Practical Guide to the Best in Building*. Initiated in 1954 and completed in 1965, the book summed up the variables in the design of a single-family home, while also serving as a critical anthology of architecture for students and laypeople. The book featured contemporary designs – including more than 75 images of Parker's own work, along with works by Frank Lloyd Wright,

Paul Rudolph, Nathaniel Owings, Eero Saarinen, George W. Brewster, John Dekoven Hill, and others – situating Parker's beliefs and work in the sweep of Modern architecture.

The design of Parker's new office workshop in Coconut Grove (1967) demonstrated another face of his developed philosophy. He had intended to build a new office from the ground up on the site of his father-in-law's homestead. Indeed, when Weyerhaeuser commissioned Parker, along with six other leading architects, to design a structure that explored innovative uses of its wood products, Parker used the opportunity to conceive the workshop as an open shed-like structure where laminated wood bents and decking were configured to make effective use of natural lighting. However, as Parker noted, "When the time for demolition arrived, sentiment for the ancient stone walls and columns was too great and a complete rebuilding began." In an act of respect that predated modern interest in preservation, Parker reconceived the project as an adaptive use of the Gifford house. As he explained, the "requirement was to demonstrate a philosophy of design: one that encompasses both the old and the new, proper use of simple but enduring materials, harmony with the site, adequate technical comfort (light, air, water), and useful spaces of changing delight."[37]

Part IV: Monumentality and social engagement (1962-1972)

To form into a whole, to unite, to bring into an unimpaired condition of integrity, of soundness, to achieve the quality or state of being complete or undivided…[W]hen such words are put into action, and when such action results in the reality of a unity between man and his environment, then will we begin to fulfill the promise implicit in the master design of our planet. – Alfred Browning Parker[38]

Having set out his first principles in *You and Architecture*, Parker refined his philosophy and strategies according to the challenges of new scales of work. By the 1960s, Parker had achieved celebrity status as a Miami architect, radio host, and newspaper columnist. He completed his largest and most lavish homes for a client list that now included real estate tycoons and public personalities,[39] as well as his own growing family. Landing large private and public commissions, Parker recast his design leadership as civic engagement. He developed expansive new idioms, including bolder exposition of architectural form, and expressionist sculpted masses that ranged from towers to earthforms, and included crystalline geometries and arboreal assemblies. He found inspiration in the vital power of natural systems and structures, and in his own power as a creator of form.

Little in Parker's past could have predicted the monumentality of his grandest homes, on prominent waterfront sites in upscale suburban enclaves. Conceived as organic architecture, yet no longer characterized by Parker's search for a Florida vernacular, these homes combined bold silhouettes, strong horizontal massing, and the use of perspective to heighten grandeur. Befitting these larger homes, Parker articulated a sense of luxury with a careful balance between public and private faces.

For Wallace Groves, the founder and patron of Freeport on Grand Bahama Island, Parker designed a broad mansion almost 200 feet in length (1959-60). Large hipped roofs tiled in blue and green (designed to reflect the waters of the Gulf Stream); taut wall surfaces of stone set in ashlar bands betray a new sense of mass and gravity, with undertones of indigenous American architectures like the Shingle Style and Wright's Prairie Style. The home respected tropicalist principles with an in-line design only one room deep, but subtle shifts in plan broke up its apparent length. At one such shift, Parker orchestrated the entry through a protected patio, a secret tropical garden at the entrance. The bold exteriors, with color palettes conceived to match the surroundings, complemented rich but subdued interiors outfitted in cypress and teak, influenced by the contemporary interest in the Japanese aesthetic called *shibui*.[40] Parker had already designed the island's resorts and clubs, its air terminal and marina, its apartments, schools and clinics, office buildings and shopping centers; yet the home transmitted a particular sense of power and ambition.

Parker's own luxurious estate in the Gables Estates section of Coral Gables (1962), *House Beautiful*'s Pace Setter 1965, went further in elaborating a sense of monumentality. Its voluminous form paralleled the waterfront, rising three stories and cleft by a 'seaway' designed to allow storm surges to pass through the home unimpeded. Broad-hipped roofs and nautical wrapping decks intersected the prow-like chimney and stair tower, making a picturesque silhouette. “Lofty prisms of glass and stone,” remarked *House Beautiful*’s new editor Sarah Tomerlin Lee,[41] commenting on the home’s heroic presence – a presence that also projected Parker’s new status.

A rural variant on these grand homes can be found in the Big B Ranch complex (1970) in Belle Glade, designed for Walter Beinecke, Jr., philanthropist and heir to the S&H Green Stamp fortune. The broad, in-line plan of the main house raised living areas over a working ground floor, reflecting its combined role as a glamorous manorial home and a working agricultural homestead. The plan of the home radiated into the open landscape of sugar cane fields and cattle grazing lands, commanding berms, ponds, exterior promenades, gardens, and dependencies.

By contrast, some of Parker’s later homes demonstrate a creeping introversion. Parker organized the Landon Residence (1965) around a paved patio and pool area that opened only partly to the waters of Biscayne Bay. A central feature of the patio was the brick hearth wall, which sprang from the living room, where it was the centerpiece of the sunken living area. Its sculptural mass provided a vital counterpoint to the informal enclosure of the patio. All around, the broad pyramidal roofs of the home hovered low over the landscape, or rose pagoda-like, one on top of the other.

Urban ecologies

Paradoxically paralleling these suburban fancies, Parker designed a succession of commercial and civic works in the 1960s that embraced the challenge of organic architecture in the city. For instance, Parker’s design of the 14-story main office of Flagler Federal Bank (1960) in downtown Miami was conceived as a singular landmark, an urban pagoda that swelled and then tapered to a skylit pyramidal roof (designed to house Parker’s workshop) crowned with a mast-like microwave tower. The outward-thrusting travertine-clad base comprised a four-story bank lobby and offices organized around a central atrium. Above, the tower would rise in weathered copper bands that protected rows of downward slanting glass. Eventually completed in 1961, the building was stripped to a simple box-like form, all sculptural qualities limited to the canopied entrances facing each street, also in weathered copper. The sculptural ambitions of the Flagler Federal headquarters were repeated over the next 20 years, nonetheless, in at least 27 suburban branch offices in South Florida.

Another type of civic ambition was evident in the Fort Lauderdale Theater (1959) on Galt Ocean Mile, designed for George Engle, an oil tycoon for whom Parker had designed the rehabilitation of the Coconut Grove Theater in 1955.[42] Its diamond-shaped 1,500-seat theater, along with the auxiliary facilities and programs, was circumscribed within a broad horizontal platform, or mat. Surrounded by promenades offering views to the city and punctuated by sky-lit lobbies, this platform cantilevered over powerful piers to form a marquee covering the simultaneous discharge of 30 cars at once.

The extreme horizontality of the Fort Lauderdale Theater may be juxtaposed with the vertical thrust of the Fort Lauderdale Tower (1965), also designed for George Engle. Certainly inspired by Wright’s 1956 Mile High Illinois tower for Chicago, this 2,000-foot tower was above all a promotional fantasy, touted as the tallest tower in the world. Accessed by bridge and flanked by low-slung concourses topped by mast-like needles, it would have surged from Fort Lauderdale’s lacework of canal and islands. The mixed-use concrete structure, a tetrahedrontripod in plan, telescoped into the sky. Rather than an expression of urban density or commercial power, it was a blade-like landmark designed as a symbol for a modern city.

Parker’s design for Quayside (1974) in North Miami, a high-density residential enclave with clusters of townhouses and mid-rise towers organized around a type of European village plan, emerged as part of the solution to promote more responsible planning, “giving the ‘feel of the land’ while conserving space by the use of common walls and vertical architecture.”[43] The plan created a sense of community, using plazas, patios, and pedestrian streets that wove picturesquely around Venetian canals and water basins.[44]

Parker’s most ambitious, if least known, urban works are his plans for Miami’s downtown waterfronts, including the Miamarina (1966), “Bay-urban” (1971), and “River-urban” (1974) projects. In the late 1960s, Parker condemned the postwar city, as he wrote and lectured extensively on the cancerous spread of unplanned sprawl around an empty urban core.[45] In these master plans for Miami, Parker asserted the responsibility of the architect to act in the public interest.

The 1966 plan to expand Bayfront Park with a new marina was, for the city, a gambit to enliven downtown with piers, yachts, and a glamorous new restaurant.[46] Parker saw Miamarina as an urban center and a mixed-use entertainment/cultural venue, an idea he shared with Constantinos Doxiadis, the Greek planner/architect commissioned to design the remainder of the Park (1966-68). He used the project to effectively extend the city into Bayfront Park.

The centerpiece of the 300-slip marina was a futurist restaurant, raised to command a view of the bay. Parker had already experimented with this type of elevated restaurant at the Sip and Sup Restaurant (1963) on North Bayshore Drive.[47] The faceted octagonal structure, constructed of heat absorbing glass prisms, was a jewel along the waterfront, itself a type of set piece. From the inside, dinner-jacketed patrons had panoramic views of the harbor. Hinged on the prismatic glass structure, Parker organized a linear public concourse including a concrete loggia that provided a raised promenade linking all parts of the complex.

Miamarina constituted a prelude to Parker's Bay-urban project, which (after the collapse of the Doxiadis plan) advocated expanding the city's waterfront parks in tandem with their redevelopment as mixed-use urban districts. Parker suggested a 'great green ribbon,' bridging the piers of the old port and connected by loggias extending from Miamarina. The plan would produce a pedestrian zone animated by public spaces, greenery, and a convention center in the waters of the bay. At either end, the park would be framed by faceted crescents of mid-rise housing in interconnected terraced structures. The linear structures would grow into crystalline formations, their battered walls framing the green space of the park. The interweaving of park space and linear megastructure would have assembled natural and man-made features into a new landscape synthesis.[48]

Parker used megastructures to achieve a sense of monumentality and urban interconnectedness. This goal reverberated in his River-urban projects, which he proposed to transform Florida Power and Light's multi-acre assemblage of transformers and other electrical infrastructure along the Miami River.[49] He produced two radical proposals, likely unsolicited, in the early 1970s. The first assembled the site's development rights into a single platform balanced on tall legs, spanning the company's transformers and riverfront industrial areas, and extending Miami's existing civic core to the water's edge.

The project explored the idea of 'integrated design,' combining commercial and civic components of all types into a single structure. It was surely influenced by the earlier proposals by Japanese Metabolists like Kenzo Tange, and perhaps even the experimental designs of Italian architect Leonardo Ricci and his students in Miami (1970), then only recently exhibited.[50] Curiously, the idea re-appears three decades later in Parker's design for a post-9/11 World Trade Center memorial for New York City. In Parker's concept, America's Memorial Bridge would have connected Manhattan to Ellis Island and Jersey City, New Jersey with a bridge-like megastructure spanning the Hudson River. The structure, inspired by the Ponte Vecchio in Florence, would have comprised more than five million square feet.

A second proposal, conceived more as landscape than structure, knit public plazas, private residential developments, retail buildings, and a new landmark tower into a mixed-use district that would span the Miami River. The existing built contours of the site, including the tall viaducts of the surrounding interstate highway, were transformed into sculpted landforms to conceal parking garages and other infrastructure. These landforms reverberated in powerful new contours that swelled from the river to break the rectilinear grid of the streets. Miami's iconic county courthouse tower was dramatically reframed as an object in this new park-like landscape.

Parker's journey from tropicalist pavilions to the collective form of megastructures was remarkable. Yet, if these urban proposals, responses to the poor effects of functionalism in planning, seem rooted in the imaginative urban visions of Team X, Aldo Van Eyck, Yona Friedman, Archigram, and the Japanese Metabolists, they should also be taken as a reassertion of Parker's organic principles at an urban scale.

Part V: Coda: A Life of Activity in Accordance with Reason (1973-2011)

Parker wound down his Miami-based practice in the 1970s. He built Windsong, his home and estate near Lincoln, Vermont, where he engaged his passion for painting and sculpture, while continuing to practice architecture. Of particular interest during this period were the St. Louis Catholic Church (1978) and Knight Residence (1979), both based on circular forms. Parker also became involved in alternative energy systems, partly in response to the energy crisis of the 1970s.[51] He and his son Robin helped found Solar Reactor Technologies Group, which developed a process to link hydrogen and electricity using hydrogen bromine (HBr), allowing large-scale energy storage from alternative sources like windmills and solar arrays. Parker's ecological ethos now merged with American environmentalism.

In 1994, Parker returned to teaching at his alma matter, the University of Florida, and moved to Gainesville permanently in 1998. Among his final projects are the two new homes he designed there for himself and his wife Euphrosyne. Skyview (1997), which was built on a narrow suburban lot, is notable for the great upper-story room that opened to the sky. Euphrosyne Isle (2004), proposed for the banks of Gainesville's Colcough Pond, was never built, but the raised Florida vernacular-inspired home demonstrated a return to traditional architectural forms.

Over the course of his career, Parker's interests shifted from local to regional to national, from private to public, from architecture to urbanism to alternative energy systems. What remained constant was an overriding discipline: a respect for nature embedded in humanism as the highest form of culture. This discipline was the foundation of a life dedicated to giving meaning to Florida's wild growth – to cultivating civility in the wilderness. "My personal need for harmony with my environment," he noted, "has resulted in a durable quest. This search is sometimes rewarded by discoveries of delight and humor. It can also become a disappointing mélange of pathos and tragedy."[52] Activist architect, writer, speaker, teacher and philosopher of his city, Parker was an original thinker whose work provided a critical and humanist counterpoint to the Modernist work of his peers; it provides a instructive counterpoint, also, to contemporary patterns of building, and to the 'green' movement in architecture that his work anticipated by more than half a century.[53]

---

1 The essay Parker penned for the first American Institute of Architects (AIA) National Convention in Miami demonstrates the architect's skepticism toward South Florida architectural conventions. Alfred Browning Parker, "We Beg to Present – Florida," *Journal of the AIA*, April 1946, p. 189.

2 'Reverence for life,' the appreciation of living things and their complex interrelation, was a cornerstone philosophy of Albert Schweitzer. "Albert Schweitzer," Wikipedia (accessed online September 7, 2016).

3 Alfred Browning Parker, "An architect views planning," 17th *Annual Florida Planning and Zoning Association Conference, Miami Beach, Florida*, 1968, p. 23.

4 Alfred Browning Parker, "Philosophy," excerpted from *Alfred Browning Parker: An Office Profile*, ca. 1971. Randolph C. Henning Parker Collection. See also "Practice Profile: Alfred Browning Parker, FAIA," *Florida Architect 21* (May-June 1971) 23-31.

5 German scientist Georg Christoph Lichtenberg quoted by Parker in *Alfred Browning Parker Sketchbook 1939-40*, p. 272, George A. Smathers Libraries, University of Florida.

6 Alfred Browning Parker, *You and Architecture: a practical guide to the best in building* (New York: Delacorte Press) 1965.

7 As Joseph M. Siry has described, "...Wright was resurgent" in the 1930s. Joseph M. Siry, "Frank Lloyd Wright's Annie M. Pfeiffer Chapel for Florida Southern College: Modernist Theology and Regional Architecture," *Journal of the Society of Architectural Historians*, 63:4 (December 2004) pp.498-539.

8 Parker's postgraduate travel defied the standard conventions of the architectural 'grand tour' of his day, typically directed toward the antiquity of the Mediterranean Sea and architectural modernism in Northern Europe . In Mexico, Parker was mentored by National Autonomous University of Mexico (UNAM) professor Dr. Federico Mariscal, a prominent figure in the teaching of cultural heritage.

9 See notes dated October 15, 1940 (Mexico City), in *Alfred Browning Parker Sketchbook 1939-40*, p. 19, George A. Smathers Libraries, University of Florida. See also *Parker to John C. Cooper Jr., Vice President, Pan American Airways, Inc., New York, March 20, 1941*, Randolph C. Henning Parker Collection. In Monica Penick, "Integrated Design: Alfred Browning Parker and the Pace Setter House Textiles, 1954," *Studies in the Decorative Arts* 16:2 (Spring–Summer 2009) pp. 91-114.

10 Early in his career, Parker documented the books he read, and those he was interested in finding. For instance, see *Sketchbook 1940*, pp. 34-39, George A. Smathers Libraries, University of Florida. Parker's personal library currently resides at the same library.

11 Penick, "Integrated Design," p. 93.

12 *Alfred Browning Parker Sketchbook 1940*, p. 82. George A. Smathers Libraries, University of Florida.

13 *Parker Sketchbook 1939-40*, p. 76.

14 According to Laseau and Tice, Wright ascribed his iconoclastic designs to intrinsic laws: "organic architecture is a natural architecture, the architecture of nature, for nature... not cherishing any preconceived form, exalting the simple laws of common sense... independence from all imposition from without." Paul Laseau and James Tice, *Frank Lloyd Wright: Between Principle and Form* (New York: Van Nostrand Reinhold) 1992, p. 4.

15 *Parker Sketchbook 1940*, p. 238.

16 Parker, "Philosophy," ca. 1971.

17 Doris Reno, "Offers plan for tropic house at $1,400," *The Miami Herald*, June 28, 1942.

18 As early as the 19th century, settlers like Ralph Munroe and William John Matheson demonstrated a deep appreciation of, and experimented with, Miami's distinctive climate and landscape. The Florida Audubon was founded in 1900, and a community of naturalists, largely centered in Coconut Grove, included journalist Marjory Stoneman Douglas and author Mabel Dorn; botanists John Kunkel Small, Charles Torrey Simpson, David Fairchild, Liberty Hyde Bailey, and Wilson Popenoe; and the forester John C. Gifford.

19 Gifford had proposed a tropical bungalow based on a synthesis of the Chinese pagoda and Cuban bohio. Dr. John C. Gifford, "Conchs and Crackers." Unattributed newspaper clipping, June 5, 1935, in the John Gifford Scrapbook, HistoryMiami Museum.

20 For background on the role of the farm in American society, I refer to Jeffrey P. Sklansky, *The Soul's Economy: Market Society and Selfhood in American Thought, 1820-1920* (Chapel Hill: The University of North Carolina Press) 2002.

21 Reno, "Offers plan for tropic house at $1,400."

22 The persiana doors used in Parker houses were fabricated by Persianas Manufacturing Company S.A., Havana, Cuba. By the 1950, multiple industries in Miami were developing modern persianas using aluminum and glass – lightweight and inexpensive 'jalousie' windows, doors, and even walls.

23 I refer to the idea of the house as environmental machine described by historian Rayner Banham. Rayner Banham, "Frank Lloyd Wright as Environmentalist," *Architectural Design* 37, April 1967, 174-77.

24 Richard Neutra's Corona School (1935) and Vladimir Ossipoff's Winne Classroom Complex at the Punahou School (1950-55) are examples.

25 Parker's use of concrete was not explicit in his first plan for the sloping site, conceived in 1948 and constituting an important pivot between his early and later work. The early design, which featured a striking cantilever toward Biscyane Bay on the second floor, retained the logic of a shed-roofed wood structure, sat on stone plinths, and made abundant use of glass and mosquito screening on the open façade facing the bay.

26 Penick, "Integrated Design," p. 91. See also Monica Penick, "The Pace Setter Houses: Livable Modernism in Postwar America," Thesis submitted to the Faculty of the Graduate School of the University of Texas at Austin, December 2007.

27 As Jonathan Massey has pointed out in his study of architect Claude Bragdon, such a decorative order could also be seen as a "critique of modern alienation," and even an expression of communitarian ideals. Jonathan Massey, *Crystal and Arabesque: Claude Bragdon, Ornament and Modern Architecture* (Pittsburgh: University of Pittsburgh Press) 2009, pp 5-18.

28 I refer in part to the tropical house ideals of Jane Drew and Maxwell Fry. "Ideally the hot-wet tropical house is a thing of point supports, a light framework allowing of the maximum of openings for adjustable louvres, windows, mosquito screening and whatever devices can be invented to induce ventilation and keep out sun, rain and insects, and ideally to cope with one or two only of these items at a time, as occasion demands... If all the walls were removed and we built within a widely over-sailing roof we would not be overdoing things. Instead of Mies van der Rohe's house of glass it would be a house of air; and given the security and absence of dust and tornadoes, given, let us say, the use of sliding walls of louvres, mesh or glass when required, what a house it would be!" Maxwell Fry and Jane Drew, *Tropical Architecture in the Humid Zone* (London: Batsford) 1956, p. 60-62.

29 Curtis Besinger, "Le Petit Grand Pavillon – American Style." *House Beautiful* 99:11 (November 1957) p. 247.

30 "The Alliance Machine Co. of Ohio Opens Offices Here: New Era Comes to Grove as Engineers Move In," *Coconut Grove Village Post* 2:9 (May, 1958) pp. 1-2.

31 Parker continued the pavilion motif for projects in the Caribbean, including a two-story pavilion for John Cameron Swayze on the Isle St. Martin, a complex of three pavilions for Robert Graham on Andros Island (1959), and at least two projects at his proposed Navy Island development near Port Antonio, in Jamaica (1963). In these island projects, complicated by topography, he posed the homes on expansive plinths, recalling the manner of Frank Lloyd Wright (at Lake Tahoe Summer Colony, for instance).

32 The later project for the Sanders Residence (1971) on Sanibel Island, comprising two star-shaped pavilions, and the Elizabeth Virrick Residence (1979) in Coconut Grove, continued to elaborate the pod house as a type.

33 Laseau and Tice, p. 117.

34 "This house is the Pace Setter for 1959 because it is THE NEXT AMERICAN HOUSE," *House Beautiful* 101:2 (February 1959) p. 73.

35 "Thoughts concerning the new sanctuary of Hope Lutheran Church," from undated brochure, Randolph C. Henning Parker Collection.

36 Parker used the factory-built wood arches to great effect in his projects, although he noted: "Wood has gotten into disfavor in the tropics, because people didn't know how to use it." "Temple Beth-El: Architect discusses his 'masterpiece,'" *Florida Builder* 35:3 (September 1980) pp. 6-7. Randolph C. Henning Parker Collection.

37 "Descriptive Data," from Design Award Program submission form, November 1968. Arva Moore Parks Collection.

38 Parker, "An architect views planning", p. 11.

39 Parker's clients in the 1960s included Wallace Groves, founder and developer of Freeport, Bahamas; Walter Beinecke, Jr., philanthropist and heir to the S&H Green Stamp fortune; Everell E. Fisher, heir to Fisher Body Company, bodymakers for General Motors; Samuel C. Johnson, head of S. C. Johnson & Son, Inc., Racine, Wisconsin; Robert Wood Johnson, chairman of Johnson & Johnson; Kirk Landon, Miami philanthropist; John Cameron Swayze, news commentator and television spokesman; James Deering Danielson, heir to the Deering Harvester Company; Jackie Gleason, American comedian; Arthur Vining Davis, American aluminum industrialist and real estate developer; and John D. MacArthur, Florida real estate developer.

40 Shibui was promoted by *House Beautiful* editor Elizabeth Gordon, who described the style as "a profound, unassuming, quiet feeling. It is unobtrusive and unostentatious. It may have hidden attainments but they are not paraded or displayed. The form is simple and must have been arrived at with an economy of means. Shibui is never complicated or contrived." "Discover Shibui, the Word for the Highest Level in Beauty," *House Beautiful* 102:8 (August 1960). As Monica Penick notes, 'Shibui' replaced 'organic' as a buzzword in the pages of *House Beautiful* in the 1960s. Penick, "The Pace Setter Houses," p. 180.

41 Sarah Tomerlin Lee, "Pace Setter 1965" *House Beautiful* 107:5 (May 1965) pp. 153-236.

42 Engle's Society of Theater Arts planned a network of performance spaces, from Coconut Grove and Fort Lauderdale to Nassau, Bahamas. The program of the Fort Lauderdale Theater included a restaurant and lounge, an art gallery, a playwrights' library, press room, theater memorabilia room, penthouse dining and dancing club, and a drama and art school. C. E. Wright, "Curtain Going Up: Plans Drawn for $2,000,000 Theater in North Fort Lauderdale," *New York Times*, November 15, 1959. See also http://janeshistorynook.blogspot.com/2015/08/plans-before-fort-lauderdales-parker.html.

43 Terry Johnson King, "Individual House is Still Part of the American Dream," *The Miami News*, August 30, 1976. See also Wayne Markham, "New American Dream Home," *Toledo Blade*, October 19, 1975.

44 Parker had previously designed medium-density patio-oriented HUD-financed public housing at Rainbow Village (1967) and Musa Isle (1972).

45 "Beauty alone in any community is completely superficial and actually not beauty at all unless that community has faced squarely and dealt properly with housing problems and a land use plan for business and industry that is rational." Parker, "The Living City," p. 4.

46 Nixon Smiley, "Miami Occupied, Pedestrianized and Greened," *Tropic Magazine*, *The Miami Herald*, January 2, 1972. See also Jack Kassewitz, "Don't give up hope – Miamarina's almost finished," *The Miami News*, May 27, 1970.

47 Following Miamarina, Parker designed a similar elevated restaurant commanding panoramic views at the Powerhouse Restaurant (1988), Otter Creek Falls, Middlebury, Vermont. He repeated the marina's prisms of glass at Abney Mills Corporate Headquarters (1965).

48 Before his 1960s interest in urban design and planning, Parker had opportunities to design larger building collectives. For instance, in Freeport, Grand Bahama Island, he designed the clubhouse, airport, medical clinic, a public school, shopping center/market, motel, apartments, bowling alley, drive-in movie theater, church, and a Barclay's bank between 1957-64. At the Navy Island project (1963) in Port Antonio, Jamaica, he used his existing home and commercial building designs to create a collage master plan.

49 In 1974, Parker was initially hired by Florida Power & Light to study the redevelopment of its riverfront properties. Calling the area "...a kind of neglected municipal cellar," and based on the proximity of high-density development to the north and south, he argued for redevelopment with a mix of all uses, including commercial, cultural, and religious. He also argued spending 10% of the project cost for demonstrations of both energy conservation and generation. *FPL Report*, Randolph C. Henning Parker Collection.

50 Italian architect-planner Leonardo Ricci, working with University of Florida students in Miami, proposed a bold 'integrated city' for one hundred thousand residents, made up of organic units of fifteen thousand residents occupying a series of raised megastructures. See Jean-Francois Lejeune, "City without Memory: Planning the Spectacle of Greater Miami," in Allan Shulman ed., *Miami Modern Metropolis: Paradise and Paradox in Midcentury Architecture and Planning* (Miami Beach: Bass Museum of Art and Glendale, CA: Balcony Press) 2009, pp. 34-59.

51 Parker described his interest in alternative fuels: "I had always had a feeling that we must change our habits... that we were really not doing good things to the planet, mainly in terms of burning hydrocarbons. Coal, gas, even wood, those are all hydrocarbons. This was the bug that was in my bonnet." http://www.miaminewtimes.com/news/the-energizer-6355341, accessed September 7, 2016.

52 Parker, "An architect views planning", p. 7.

53 Ibid, p. 8.

54 The author wishes to acknowledge the scholarship and research embodied in Randolph C. Henning's *The Architecture of Alfred Browning Parker: Miami's Maverick Modernist* (Gainesville: University Press of Florida) 2011.

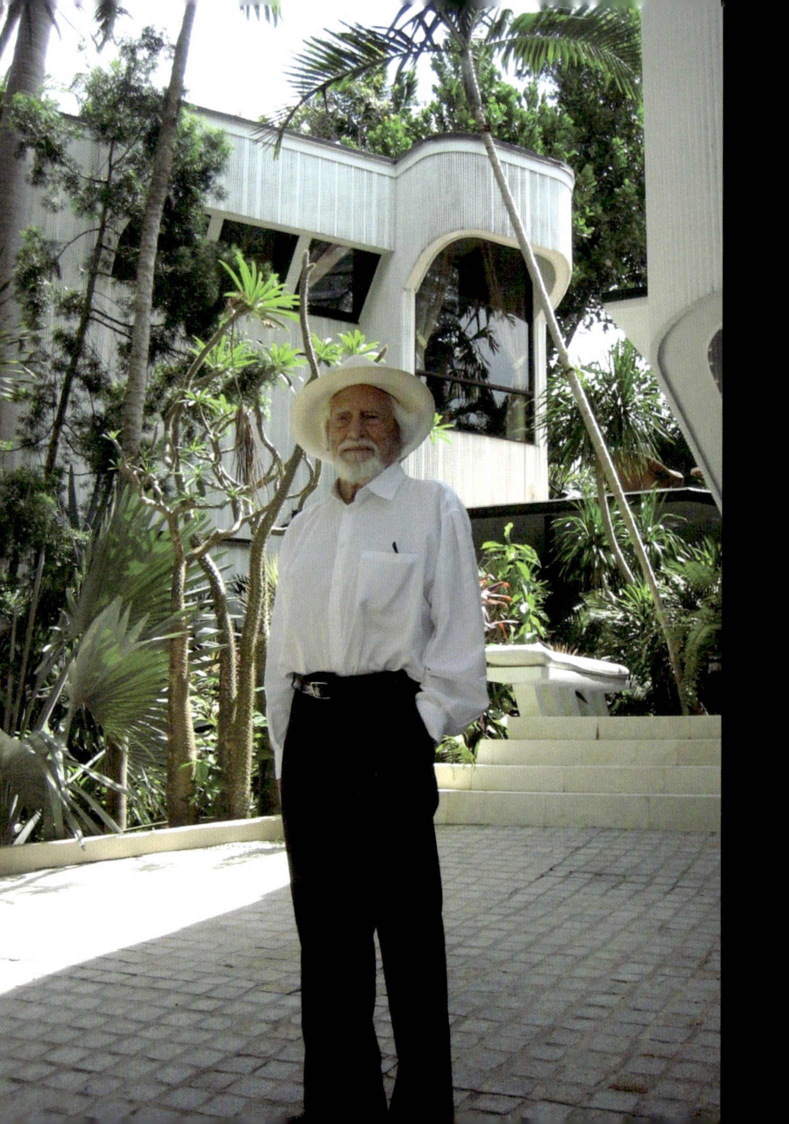

The Alfred Browning Parker I Knew

Randolph C. Henning

Because of my never ending search for everything Frank Lloyd Wright, it was inevitable that my path would cross with that of Alfred Browning Parker (1916-2011). After all, in 1970, it was his book *You and Architecture* that enlivened my interest in architecture. Thirteen years later, I met him for the first time, on the morning of August 6, 1983. I was pursuing research on Frank Lloyd Wright's work in Florida and I wanted to learn more about Parker's personal experiences with Wright. I traveled the 35 miles from Fort Lauderdale to Coconut Grove and met him at his home, "Woodsong," on Seminole Street. He spoke to me for several hours in his sun-filled study up among the trees (to me, it felt more like a tree fort). I came away enamored with Parker, along with my copy of *You and Architecture* inscribed "For Randolph C. Henning, who shares my admiration for FLLW." I didn't know it then, but the seed had been planted that would eventually sprout 28 years later, in the form of my book, *The Architecture of Alfred Browning Parker: Miami's Maverick Modernist*.

Our paths crossed again a year after our first meeting, when we shared the dais at the opening event of a Frank Lloyd Wright exhibition held at the Bass Museum of Art in Miami Beach, Florida. Parker was charismatic, romancing and captivating the crowd, the star of the show. I knew then that I needed to learn more about this man and his celebrity (now the popular term is "starchitect"). Thereafter, slowly but surely, we corresponded (I had moved to North Carolina in 1987) while I struggled with my research on Wright in Florida, mostly having to do with the lack of cooperation from Florida Southern College. I had wanted to include a final chapter in that book on Florida-based architects whose work was inspired by Wright's organic philosophy. It finally dawned on me: why not author an entire monograph on the creative life work of Alfred Browning Parker. It hadn't been done and his work certainly deserved to be seen and appreciated by a larger audience. I approached Parker on May 5, 1992 and asked for his endorsement. Without hesitation, he told me he would help any way he could.

During the next 19 years, until the book was published (sadly, three months after his death on March 11, 2011), I was Parker's official "biographer" (his characterization, not mine). While it humbled and made me proud at the same time, completing the task at the level his life and work deserved was a huge responsibility. He freely introduced me to others as his biographer with conviction. When asked when I was going to complete the task, he would defend my plodding progress, saying that I was an architect first and would complete the book in due time. He never questioned that it would get done. Nor did he try to intervene, steer me one way or another, nor ask to review my work. He trusted me.

I'm sure that the last 19 years of Parker's life, while I was working on the book, were different from the previous 75. His heyday as an architect with a thriving office had passed, but these last years were by no means retirement. By 1983, he had relocated his architectural office to his home. He would work on a couple of dozen architectural projects (of which only a handful were built) as compared to well over 500 completed since he opened his office on January 1, 1946. By the 1980s Parker had shifted his attention to renewable and alternate energy sources and he focused on his Solar Reactor Corporation. After living through the devastating Hurricane Andrew in 1992, and tiring of the rat race of South Florida, he sold Woodsong in 1993 and moved permanently to "Windsong," his home and studio annex in Vermont.

Alfred Browning Parker, December, 2007
Photograph © Dereck Winning
Courtesy Randolph C. Henning

However, by 1994 he returned to his alma mater, the University of Florida, joining the faculty and teaching graduate students in architecture. While teaching, he designed Skyview and Euphrosyne Isle, his eighth and ninth homes as architect, builder, and owner. He also produced drawings of a visionary project in response to the 9/11 tragedy in New York City, replacing the tall twin towers with a horizontal mega-structure spanning the Hudson River from the World Trade Center site in Manhattan to New Jersey and Ellis Island (a Ponte Vecchio on steroids). On parallel tracks he wrote his memoirs, started a book on former University of Florida architecture dean Rudolph Weaver, produced wood sculptures, painted, and created paper collages.

As he aged, Parker avoided talking about his past. He lived in the present and was excited about the future. I asked him once what might be some of the most significant moments in his life. His answer was, "In my life, it's always the next one." He told me that he truly couldn't wait to get up every morning, always looking ahead to the next challenge, working on the next idea, enjoying the search for solutions. In his memoir, privately printed in 2010 by the School of Architecture at the University of Florida, he wrote:

There is a danger in trying to live up to your reputation. It is more prudent to ask a question – What are you doing tomorrow? – The answer – 'Better than I did yesterday.' – A mind is to use. Dormancy is not tolerable. Go to the end of your life all used up.

Of course, he made an exception to discuss the past with me. He knew I needed his input and he was always there to answer my questions, via my visits to Coconut Grove, Vermont, or Gainesville, or through our continuous correspondence. He passionately and energetically recalled so much more than I ever thought he would about his past. When he spoke of his work, he more often spoke about his clients than about the architecture. It was obvious he developed close relationships with his clients; he recognized that the client gave purpose and life to his architecture.

His past architectural successes also took a less important role to him in those later years. As a youth, he loved playing outdoors in the tropical environment of South Florida. In the mid-1940s, he began to formalize his concern for the environment. One of his mentors was Dr. John C. Gifford, a pioneering ecologist and professor in tropical forestry at the University of Miami (his other mentors being Rudolph Weaver, the first director of the University of Florida's School of Architecture and Allied Arts, and Frank Lloyd Wright). Gifford wrote about creating a tropical subsistence homestead and this interested the young Parker. The fuel crisis in the 1970s prompted in Parker a commitment to be part of the evolution of an energy conversion system to eliminate the need for fossil fuels. In the years I knew him, he preferred to talk in public about the conservation of human and environmental resources, the development of alternate clean energy resources, and the need to understand better our incredibly beautifully balanced eco-system. However, his architectural successes were hard for him to avoid, as even late in life he continued to be recognized as Florida's most distinguished architect, receiving awards, honors, and accolades. In the two years before his death, he received the AIA Miami's prestigious Lifetime Achievement Award (in 2010) and was a Living Legends Honoree by the Dade Heritage Trust (in 2011). He is still recognized as Florida's best architect, ever.

I often thought that he would outlive me. His energy and passion seemed to get stronger over the years. I more often than not came away from our visits shaking my head, wondering,"How does he do it?" I was totally impressed with his vim, vigor and vitality. He was like the Eveready Energizer Bunny. However, that didn't mean he wasn't facing his mortality. Like most things he did in life, he faced his eventual departure straight on. In fact, in 1998, he penned his own 5-paragraph obituary, ending with, "As he expired, those witnessing his passing believe they heard him whisper, 'Life is generous.'" It proved to be 13 years premature. In 2003 he wrote to me:

I'm not as good as once I was, but rejoice in what remains. I can't see as once I saw, but there is much I'd rather not see. I don't hear as once I heard, but there is much I'd rather miss. I can't bite like once I could, but dentists are remarkable. I can't propagate like once I could, but my genes are spread enough. My heart doesn't beat as strong as before, but it has served me well. I count my blessings and am content.

Alfred Browning Parker was a creative genius. Frank Lloyd Wright, who was known to be a bit stingy with public praise of other architects, recognized this when he wrote on Parker's Royal Road house in a 1953 issue of *House Beautiful* magazine: "This Florida house aims at the highest goal to which architecture may aspire: organic architecture."

Parker was a visionary, but his visionary ideas were always based in reality. While he was a confident man, he was not arrogant. He had an ego, but wasn't an egotist. He was honest, generous, and gracious. He was as respectful as he was respected. He was proud, but far from a narcissist. His sense of humor, his passion, and his love for life, were always present. In exchange for the gift of life, he believed that each person has a responsibility to leave the world a better place. He wondered, hoped, and by the end of his life, I'm sure, he knew, he had succeeded (with a wink and a nod).

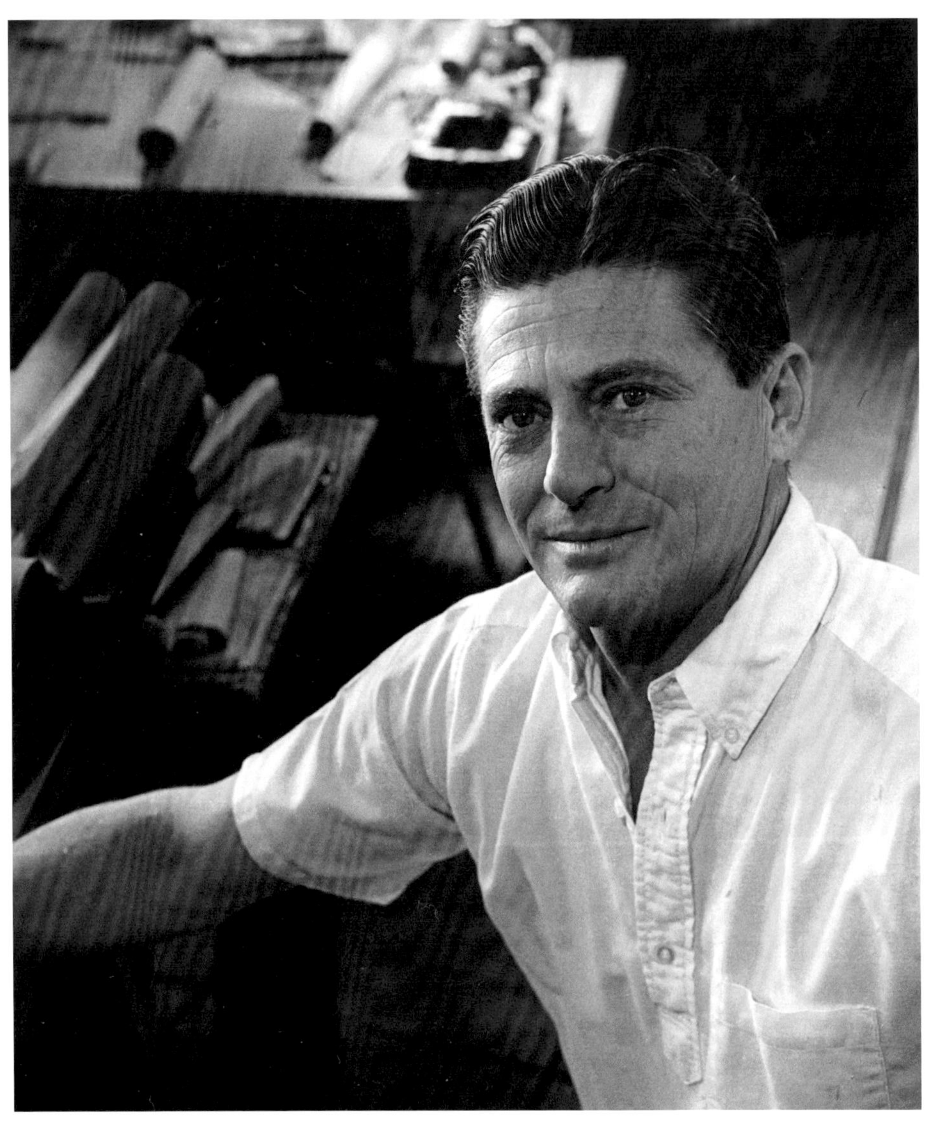

Alfred Browning Parker, undated
B&W vintage photograph, 10"x 8"
Courtesy of Randolph C. Henning

Philosophy, ca. 1971
Excerpt from *Alfred Browning Parker: An Office Profile*
Courtesy of Randolph C. Henning

From an early acquaintance with the writings of Whitman, Thoreau, Shakespeare and Alger, the possibilities of life were sensed; from the works of Szekely, Korzybski and Gifford an inkling absorbed of ecological destiny. Although I am a true believer in change I find principles are less subject to change. Over four years ago I was asked to write my philosophy which was published in the May 1967 issue of the Florida Architect.

It is my belief that man must constantly seek to live harmoniously in his environment. He must be a conservationist of both human and material resources. It sometimes appears that we are children playing with our planet rather than maturing heirs to an incredibly beautiful balanced system. We must apply the accumulated knowledge of many disciplines to our mutual problems. Educated and experienced as an architect I feel an obligation to utilize whatever skill I possess to this cause.

In our democracy we have the opportunity to aspire to nobility in our thoughts and to demonstrate high purpose in our actions. While we may not be equal in our capabilities we are the same in the freedom that we possess.

Some time ago I established these principles as guides:

BUILD STRONGLY.

BUILD AS DIRECTLY AS POSSIBLE WITH NO COMPLICATIONS.

USE THE MATERIALS AT HAND AND KEEP THESE AS FEW AS YOU CAN.

LET YOUR BUILDING LOVE ITS SITE AND GLORIFY ITS CLIMATE.

DESIGN FOR USE – MAKE IT BEAUTIFUL.

While I have not always been successful in fulfilling these ideals I have not changed my mind as to their validity. Paradoxically, change is a sure law of the universe. To recognize this law is a sign of maturity in Architecture. To be aware of the aging process in our designs and constructions is a necessity of architecture. The maintenance and durability of a structure depend upon the selection of materials and the manner in which they are assembled.

Communication is a problem of our age, greater for some than others, but germane to any creative process. It is my desire to inspire both clients and craftsmen to the best efforts of which we are capable. Since I dislike irritation and controversy it becomes essential for me to prepare contract documents that are clear and complete. While my preference among the philosophers is for the humanists, in the sciences I have always possessed an interest in ecology. I delight in man's search to attune himself to the rhythms of the universe and in our efforts to regenerate our environment.

As a beginner I needed clients. Now I must be careful not to undertake too much. Opportunities may be so abundant as to prevent progress. It is rarely ever that quantity prevails over quality. As I age my respect for material accomplishments diminishes. To produce architecture demands the stamina, endurance, energy, enthusiasm and optimistic outlook that springs from good health.

I hope for an architectural future that is a continuous attempt to harmonize buildings with our environment. Our ego in creative work is not relinquished easily or quickly but we need much less of "look at me" construction.

This philosophy does not lead to individual buildings sensationally formed. It does require a sensitive acknowledgment of the entire community. The individual creativity of the designer will be challenged by a more difficult job and he will be required to exercise greater discipline in his work. Buildings should not stand out in the childish sense of blatant commercialism that we see around us today. We must seek a much higher level of achievement.

We should judge architecture by how well it serves the growth of human spirit. Architecture is for the use and delight of the family of man happily at home on earth.

How satisfying to dwell in communities where unity of design prevails; where buildings are so at one with the environment that they are actually difficult to see; where trees, shrubs, flowers, and grass prevail (even weeds since they are only plants out of place and, here, all would be in harmony); where no signs, poles or wires intruded; where fresh air and fresh water seem the least heritage we can pass to the next generation (at present we discuss the high cost of ending pollution as though we had a choice. When your appendix has ruptured, do you pause to bargain with the surgeon?); where mankind grows closer to his infinite potential; where stagnation of the human soul is constantly being reduced and replaced by wisdom, vision and courage.

These are laudable goals. I will be the first to admit my inability to completely accomplish this dream, but then my ambitions have always been beyond my capacities. Some of us must try, and I prefer to be counted among those who do.

Part I

In search of a discipline

(1935-1941)

Industrial port, Sweden, August 18, 1939
Pencil on paper, 10 ¼" x 6 ½"
George A. Smathers Libraries, University of Florida

Woman in a red dress, Sweden, February 18, 1940
Colored pencil on board, 9 ¼" x 7 ¾"
George A. Smathers Libraries, University of Florida

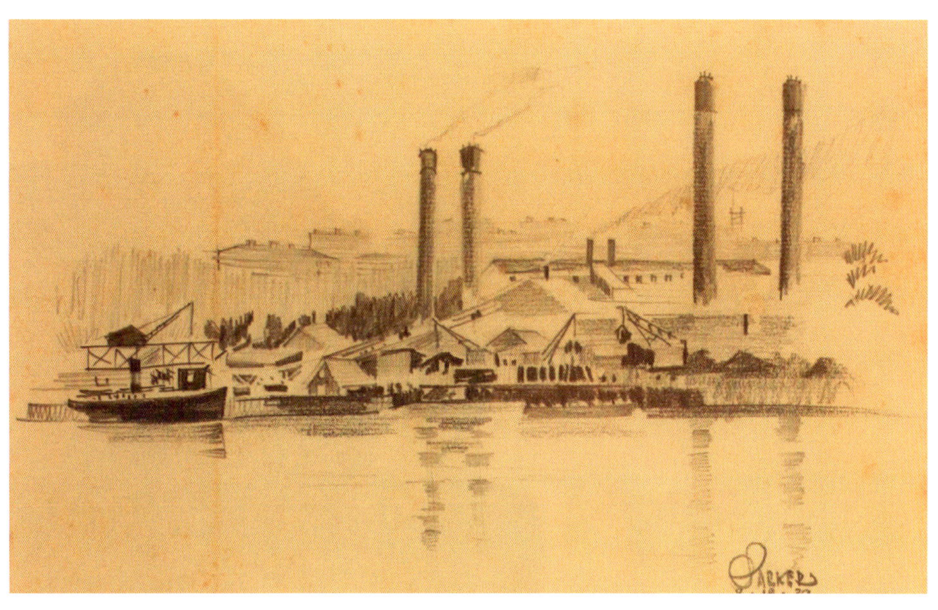

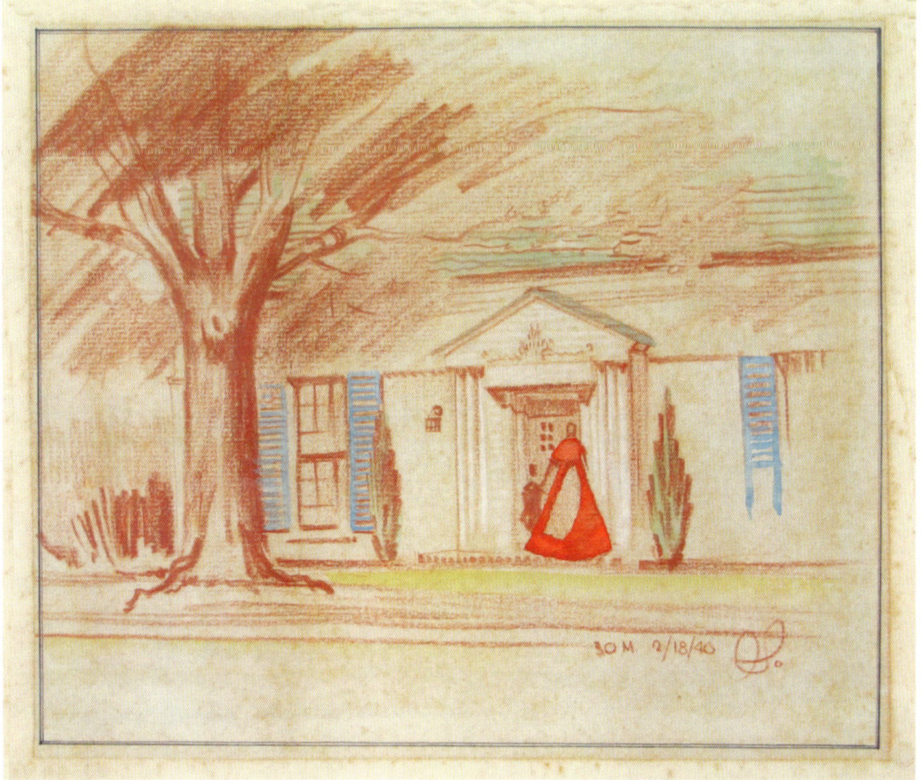

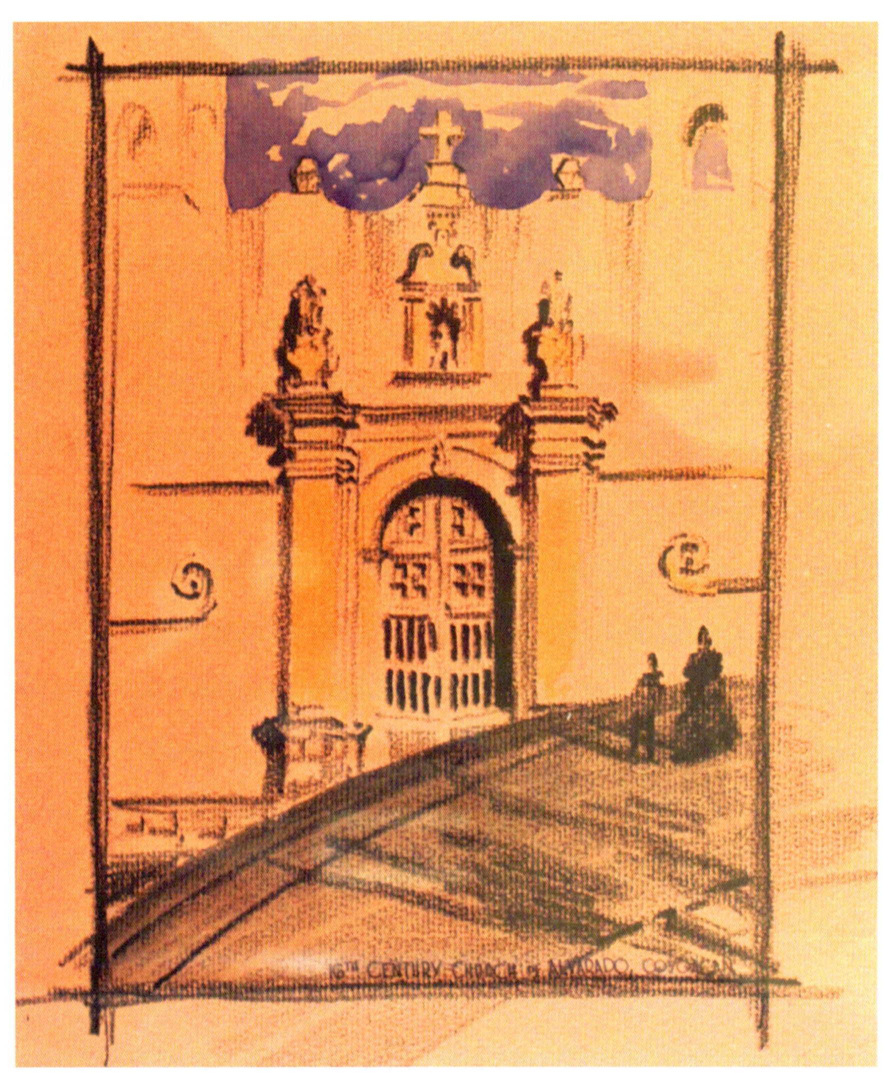

16th Century church at Amadado, Coyoacán, Mexico, 1940
Pencil, colored pencil, and watercolor on paper, 10" x 13"
George A. Smathers Libraries, University of Florida

Sketches of details, June 28, 1940
Excerpt from Alfred Browning Parker sketchbook
Ink on paper
George A. Smathers Libraries, University of Florida

Street scene, Mexico, 1940
Ink on paper, 8 ⅝" x 10 ⅝"
George A. Smathers Libraries, University of Florida

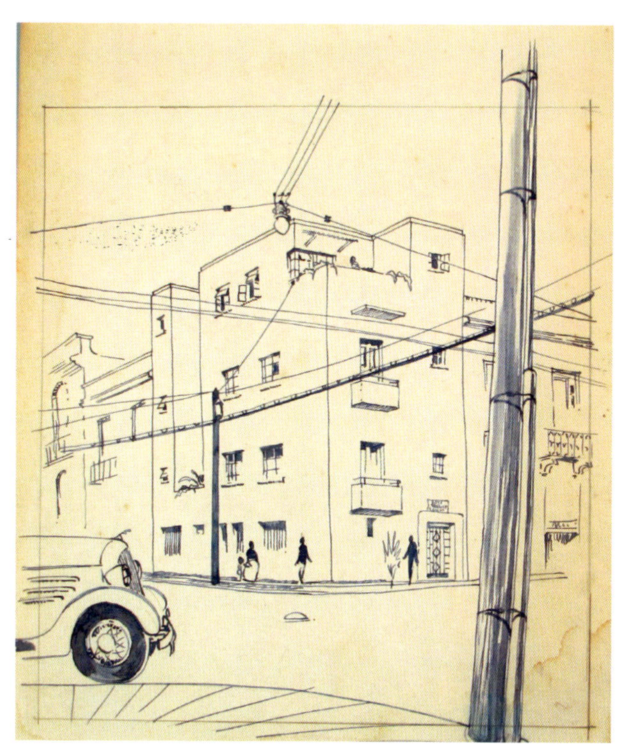

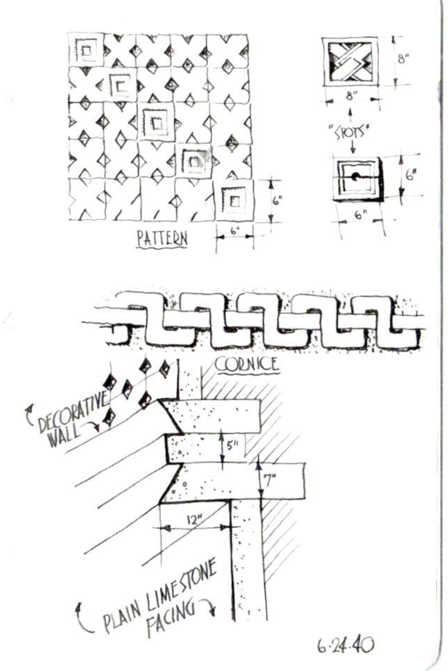
8"
8"
"SPOTS"
6"
6"
6"
PATTERN
6"
CORNICE
DECORATIVE WALL
5"
7"
12"
PLAIN LIMESTONE FACING
6·24·40

Part II
Manifestos of Self-Sufficiency (1942-1951)

Parker Residence under construction, Coconut Grove, 1943
B&W vintage photograph, 4 ½" x 6 ½"
George A. Smathers Libraries, University of Florida

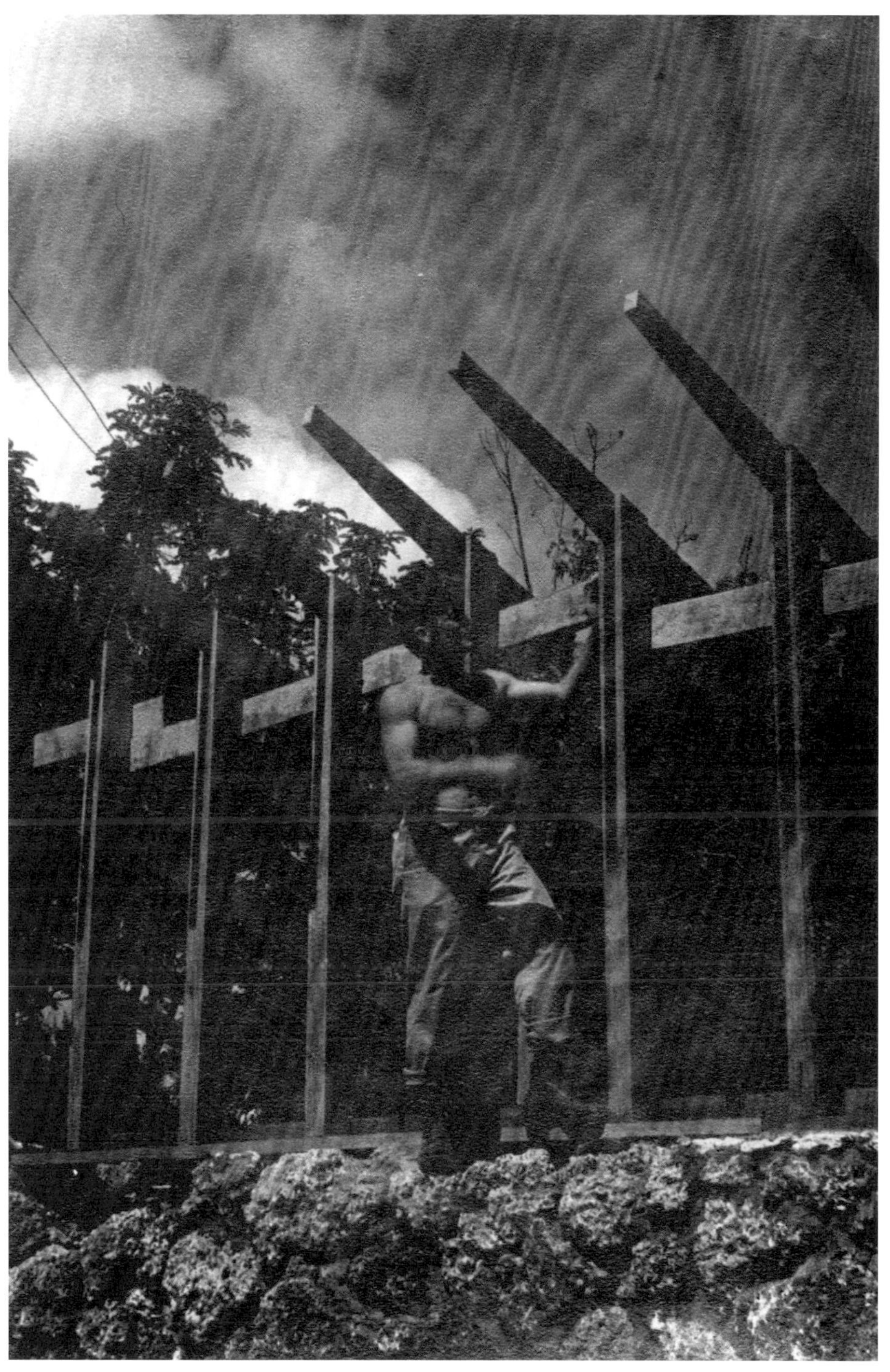

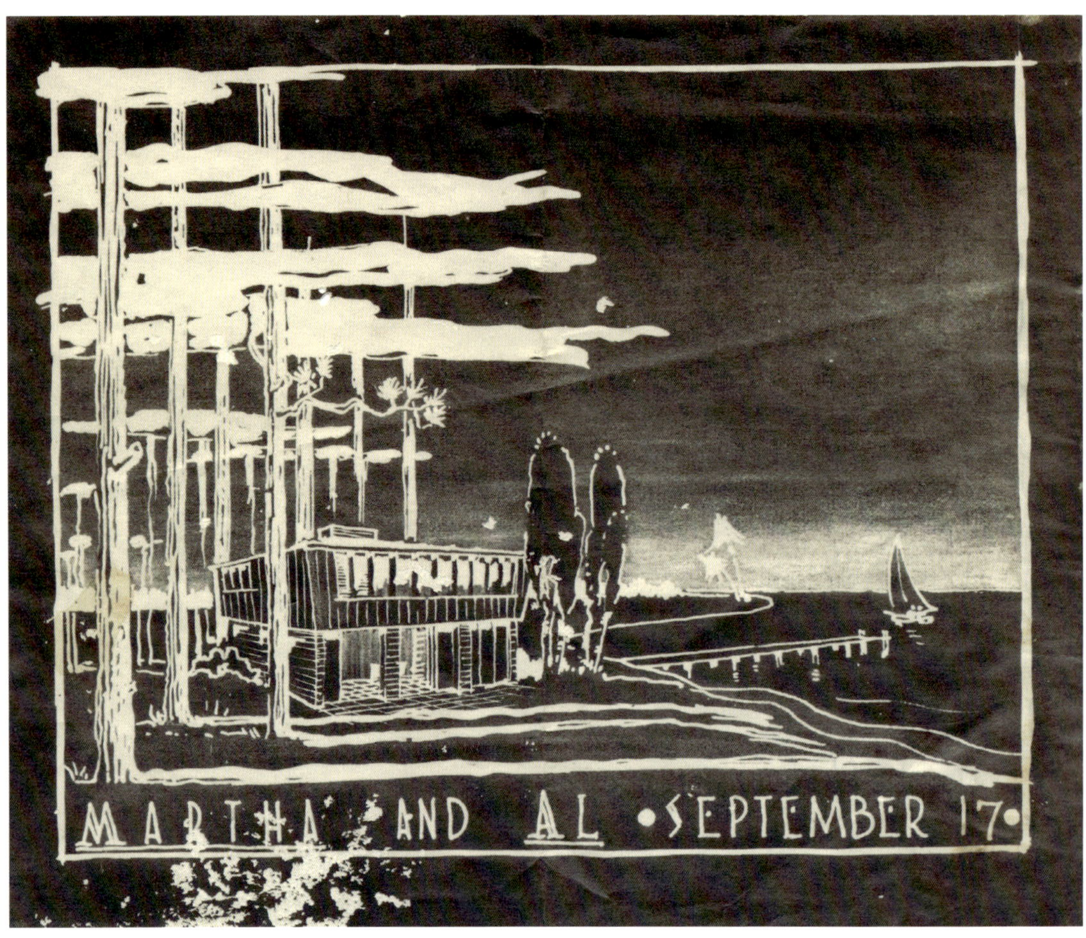

Wedding announcement featuring the Tropical Subsistence Homestead, 1942 (unbuilt)
Perspective rendering
Reproduction
Courtesy of Randolph C. Henning

Parker Residence, Coconut Grove, 1943
Living area
B&W vintage photograph, 10″ x 8″
George A. Smathers Libraries, University of Florida

Parker Residence, Coconut Grove, 1943
B&W vintage photograph, 5″ x 4″
George A. Smathers Libraries, University of Florida

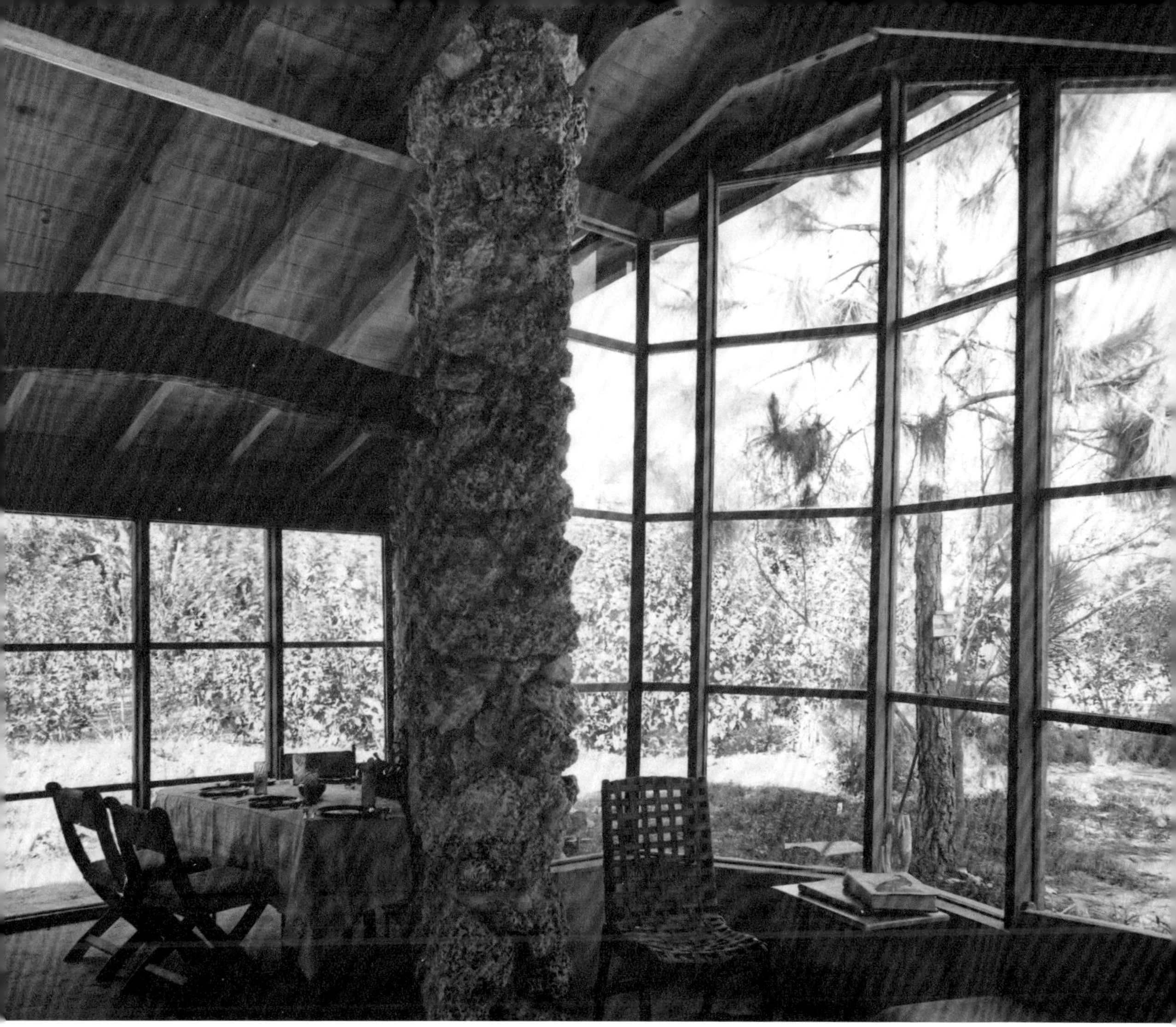

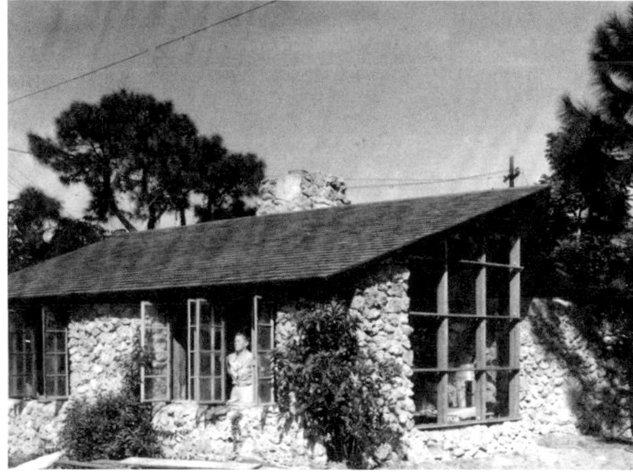

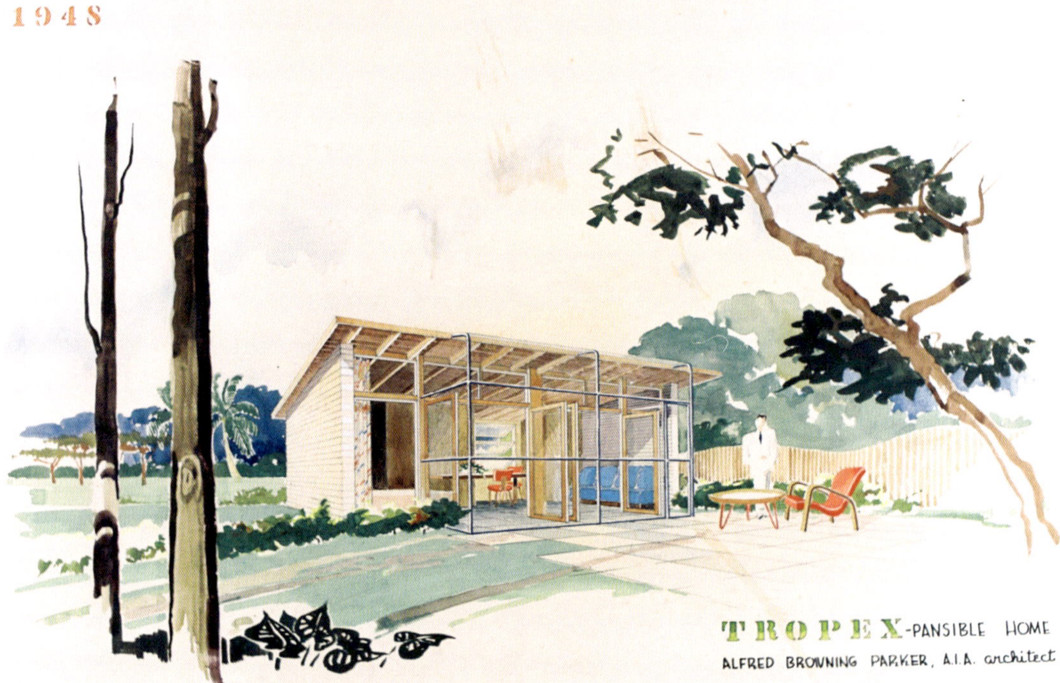

Tropex-pansible Home, 1948 (unbuilt)
Rendering
Watercolor on board, 30" x 20"
George A. Smathers Libraries, University of Florida

Parker Residence, Gainesville, 1946
B&W vintage photograph, 10" x 8"
Courtesy of Randolph C. Henning

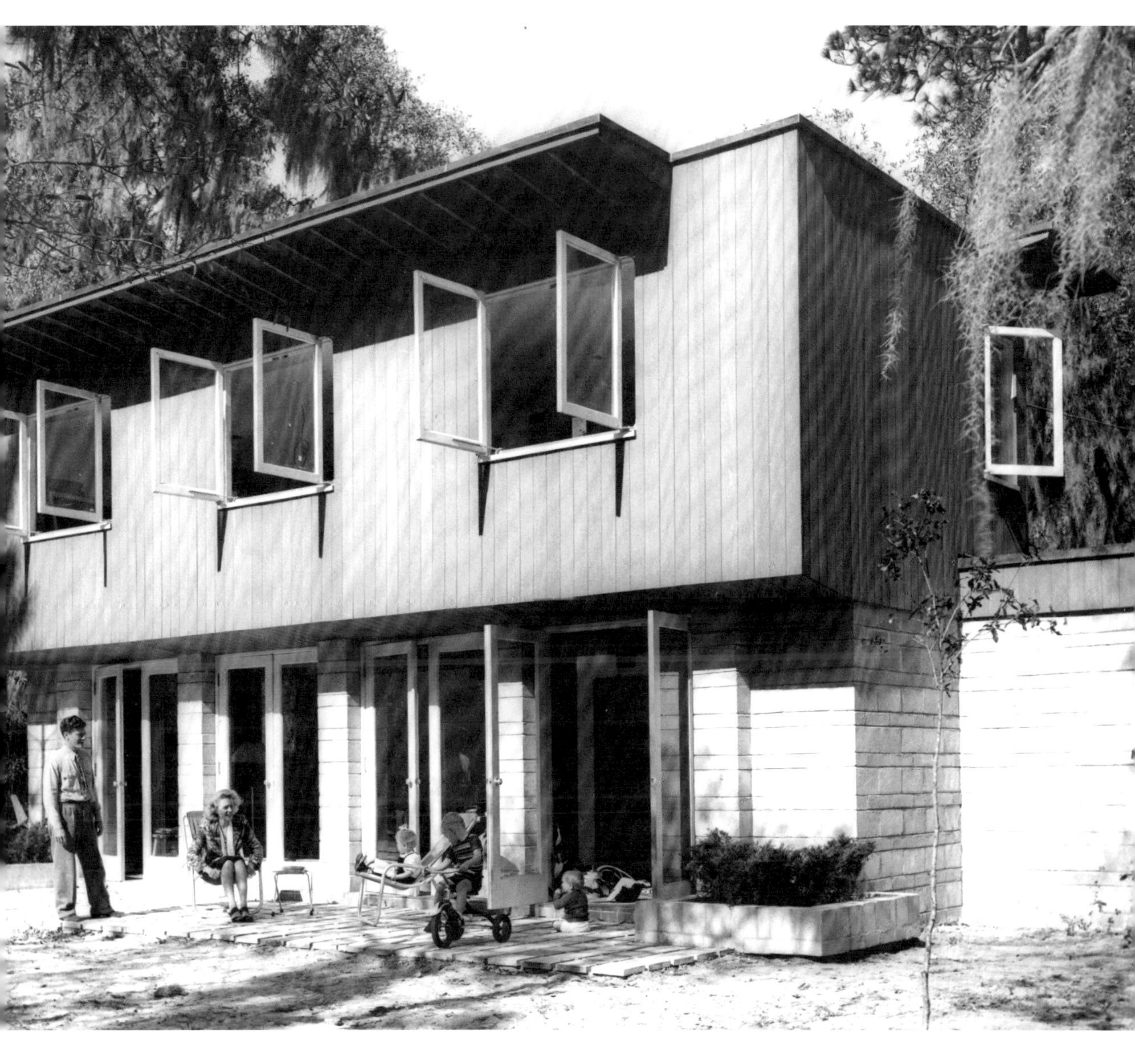

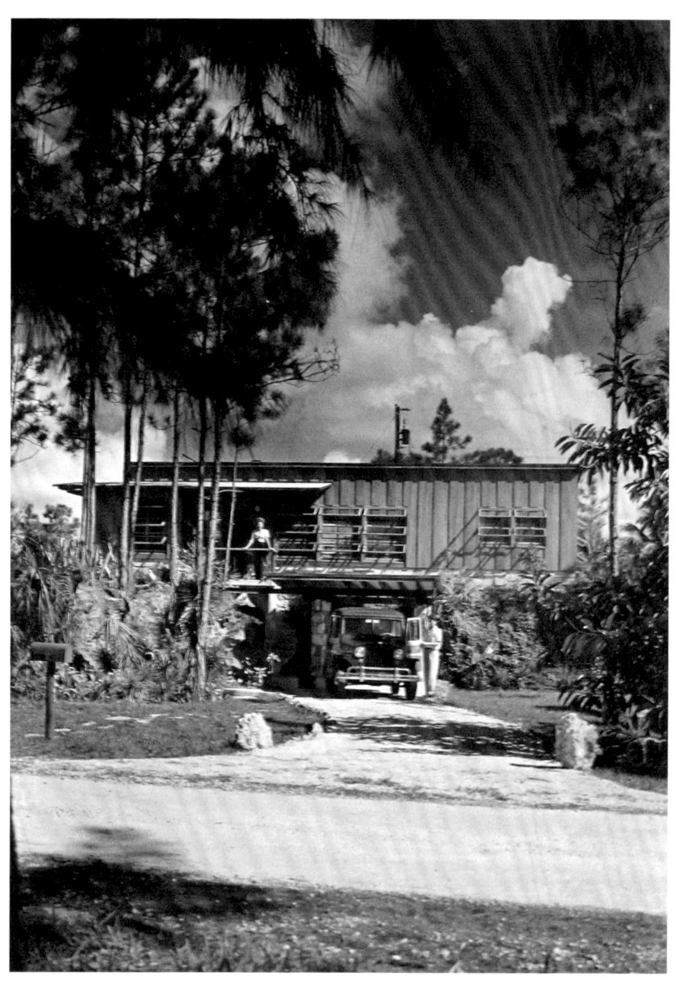

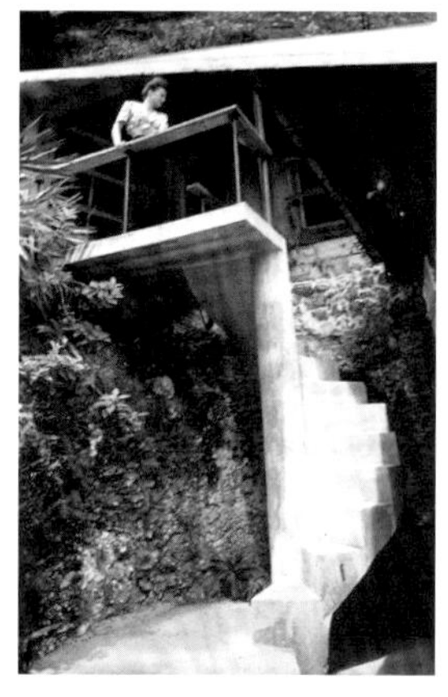

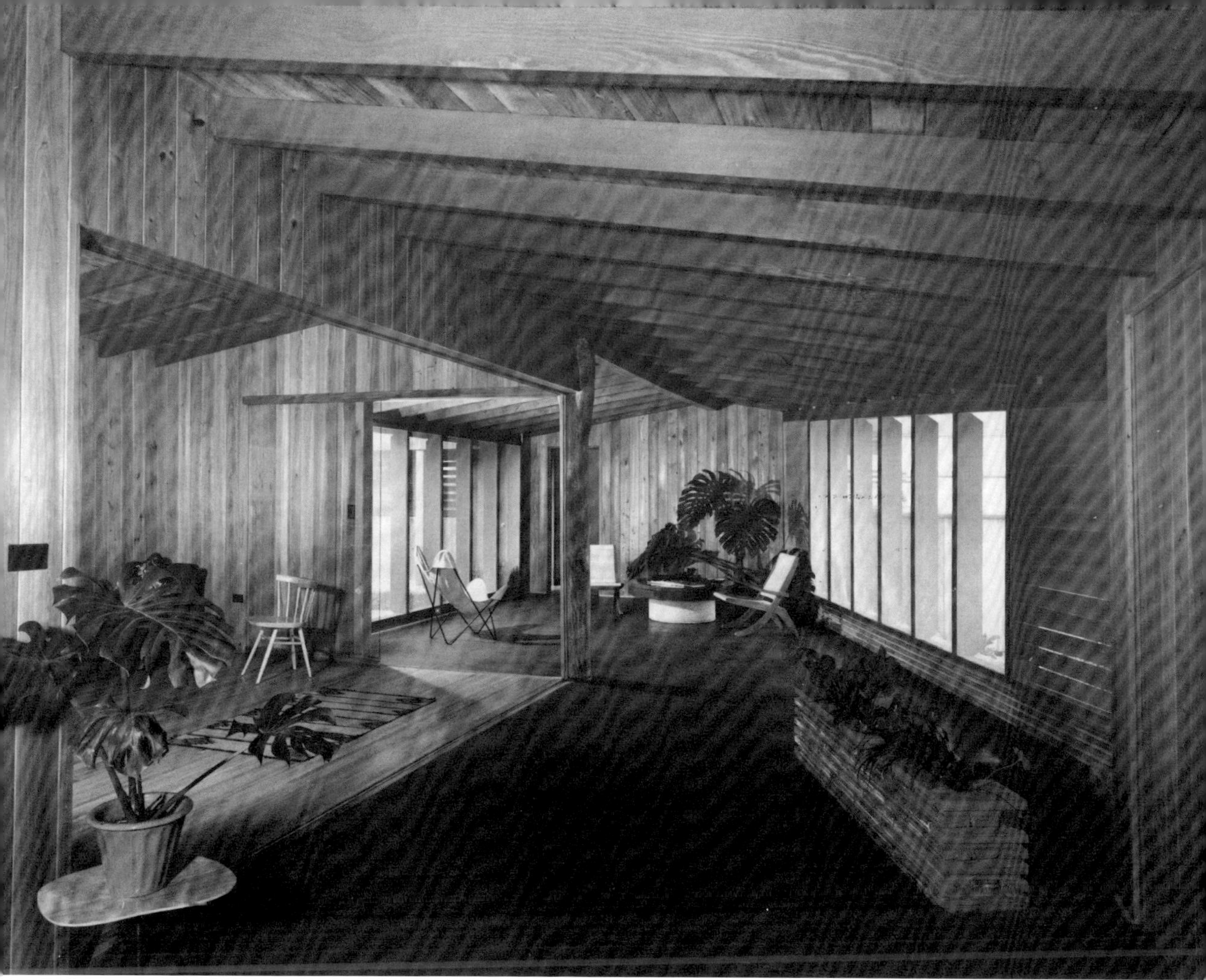

Hopwood Residence, Coconut Grove, 1946
B&W vintage photograph, 10 ½″ x 13 ⅜″
Photograph © Rodney McCoy Morgan/Photolog
George A. Smathers Libraries, University of Florida

Hopwood Residence, Coconut Grove, 1946
Exterior stair and balcony
B&W vintage photograph, 10 ½″ x 13 ⅜″
Photograph © Rodney McCoy Morgan/Photolog
George A. Smathers Libraries, University of Florida

Parker Residence (Rocks and Short Pines), Miami, 1949
Living area and porch
B&W vintage photograph, 9 ½″ x 7″
Photograph © Rudi Rada/Rada Photography
George A. Smathers Libraries, University of Florida

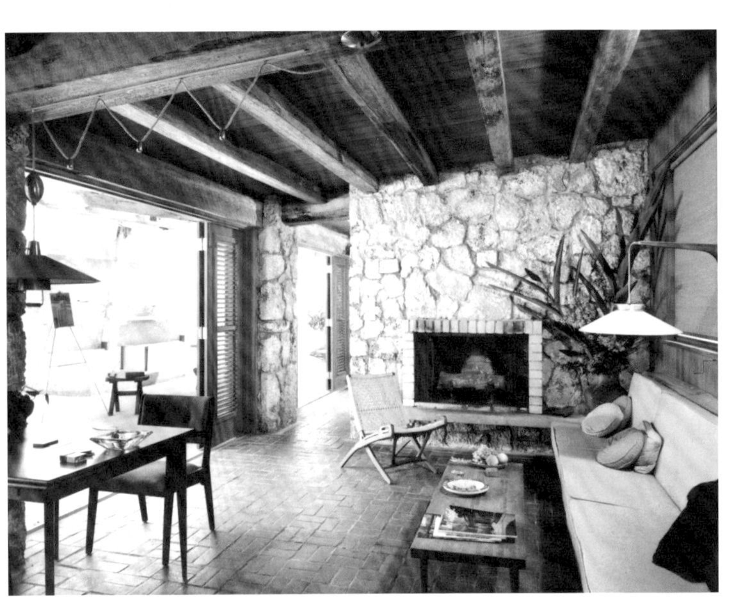

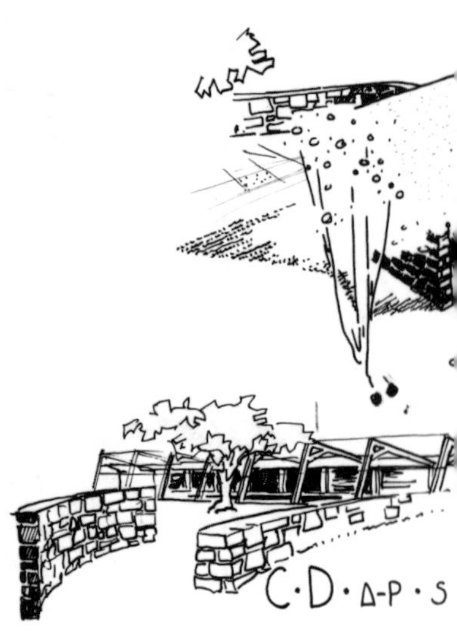
C·D·Δ-P·S

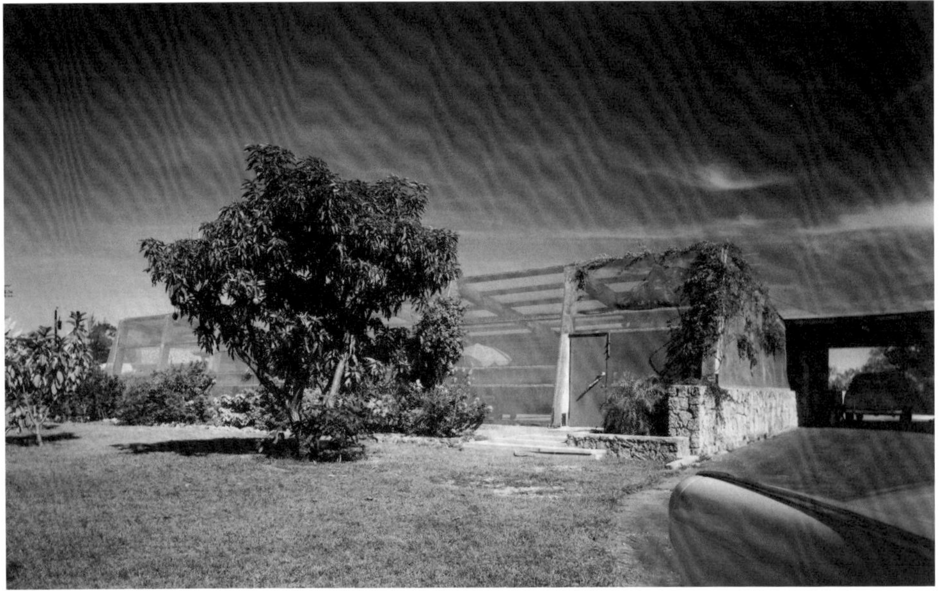

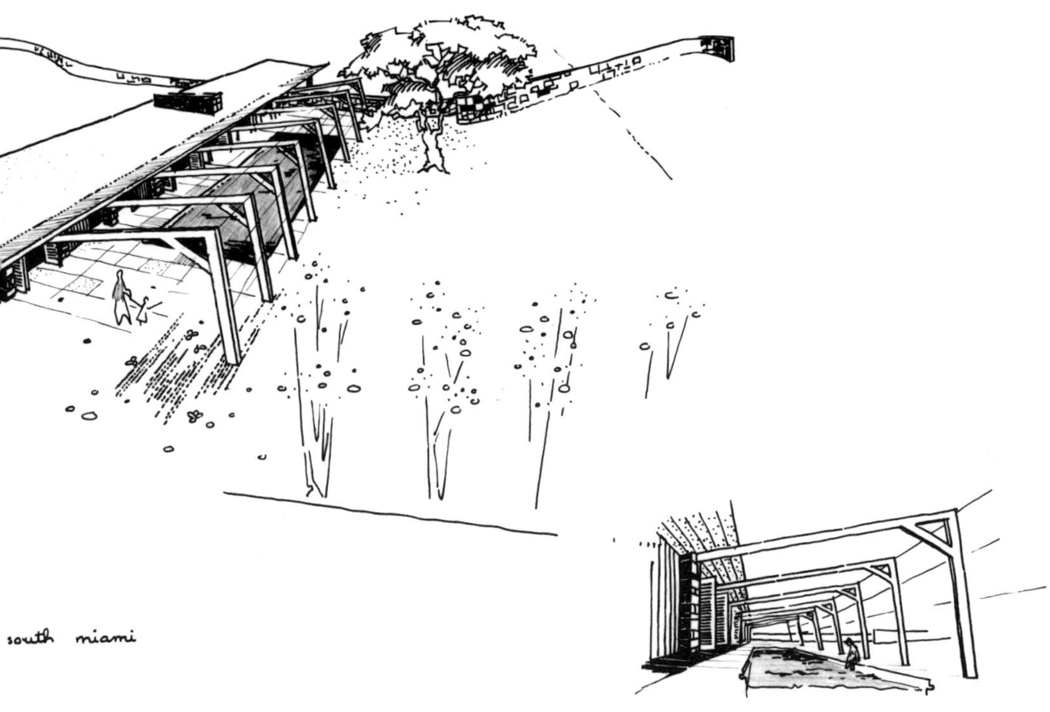

Litsey Residence, South Miami, 1952
Living room
B&W vintage photograph, 10″ x 8″
Photograph © Ezra Stoller/ESTO
George A. Smathers Libraries, University of Florida

Litsey Residence, South Miami, 1952
Microfilm
George A. Smathers Libraries, University of Florida

Litsey Residence, South Miami, 1952
B&W vintage photograph, 10″ x 8″
Photograph © Ezra Stoller/ESTO
George A. Smathers Libraries, University of Florida

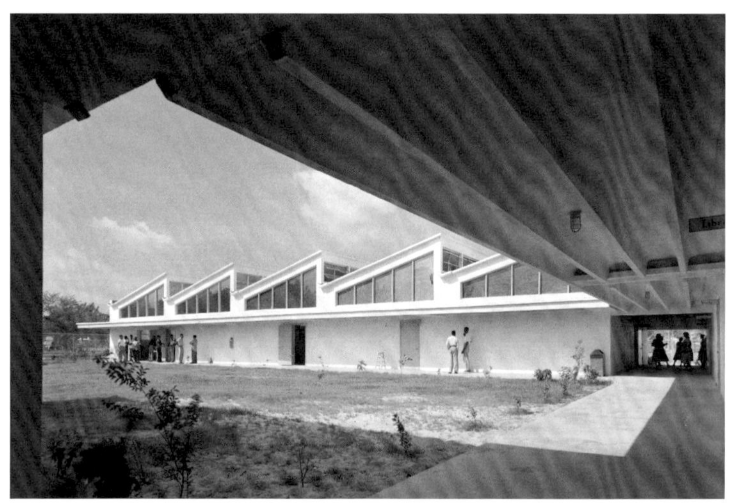

George Washington Carver School, Coral Gables, 1949
Art Studios
B&W vintage photograph, 13 ¼" x 8 ⅝"
Photograph © Ezra Stoller/ESTO
George A. Smathers Libraries, University of Florida

George Washington Carver School, Coral Gables, 1949
Classroom
B&W vintage photograph, 12 ¾" x 10 ¼"
Photograph © Ezra Stoller/ESTO
George A. Smathers Libraries, University of Florida

George Washington Carver School, Coral Gables, 1949
Section perspective through classroom
Microfilm
George A. Smathers Libraries, University of Florida

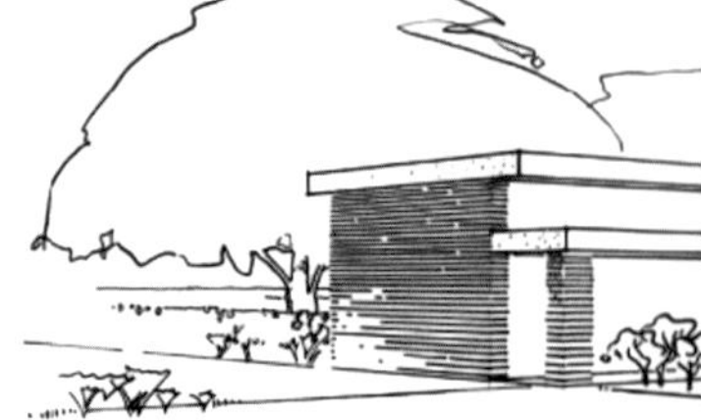

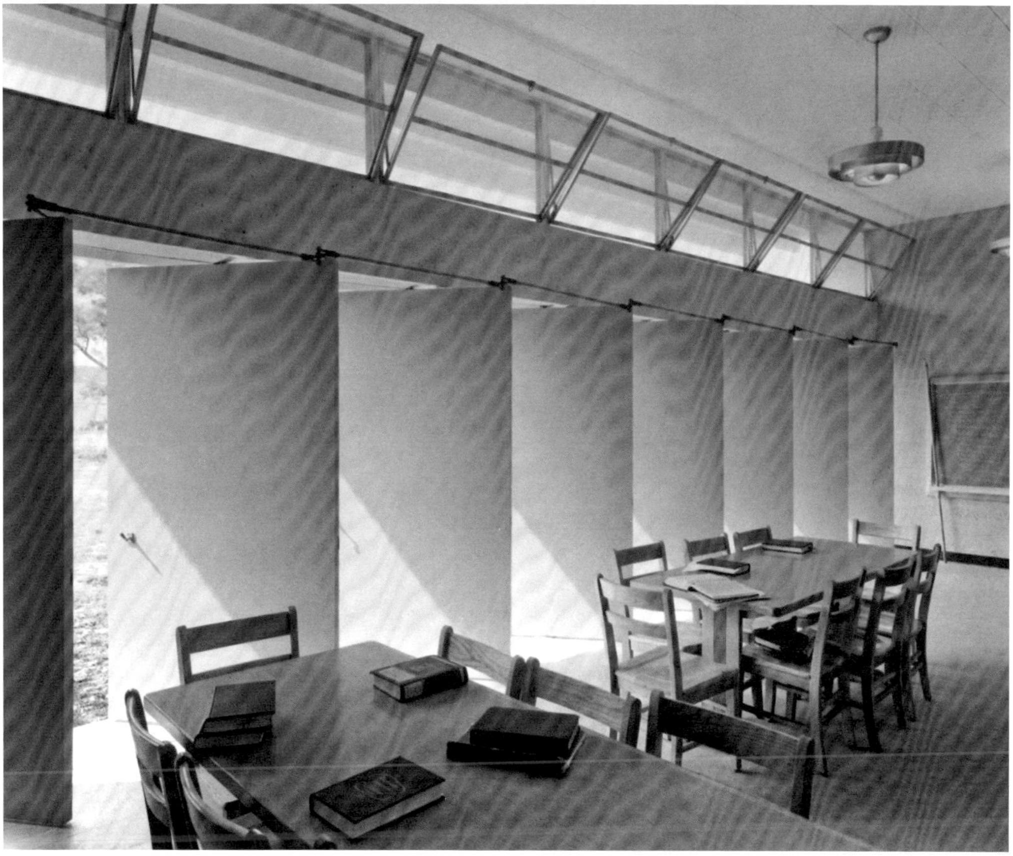

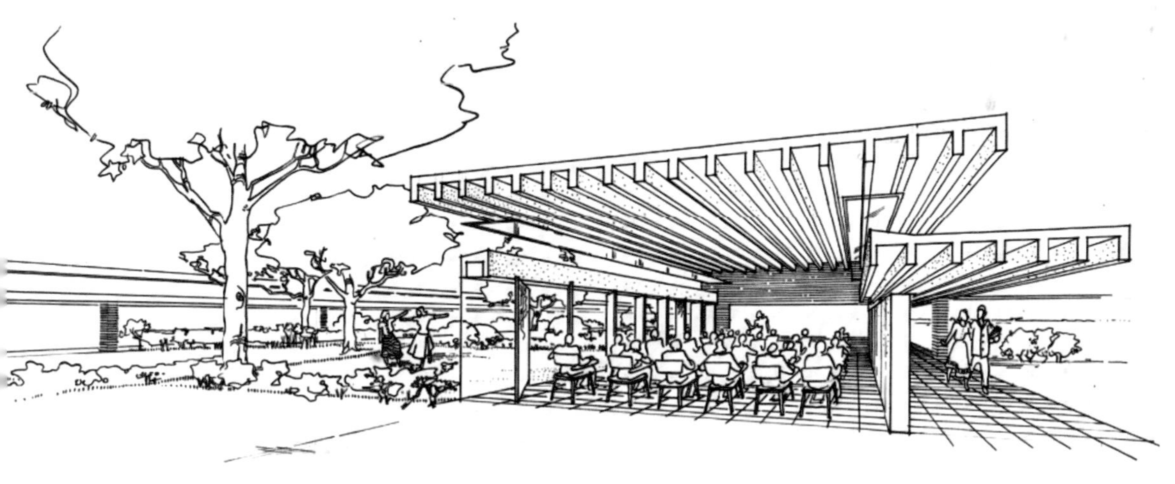

Part III
Regional and Modern
(1952-1961)

Parker Residence, Coconut Grove, 1949
Perspective rendering of preliminary concept
Watercolor on museum board, 22” x 16”
Courtesy of Euphrosyne Parker and Family

Parker Residence, Coconut Grove, 1950
Perspective rendering of final concept
Reproduction
Courtesy of Robin Parker

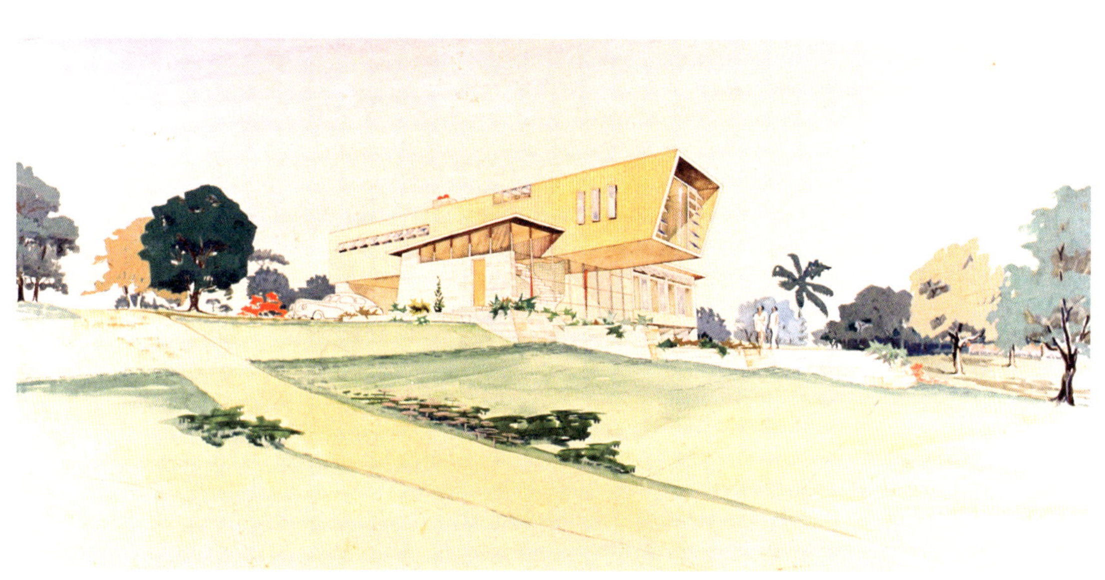

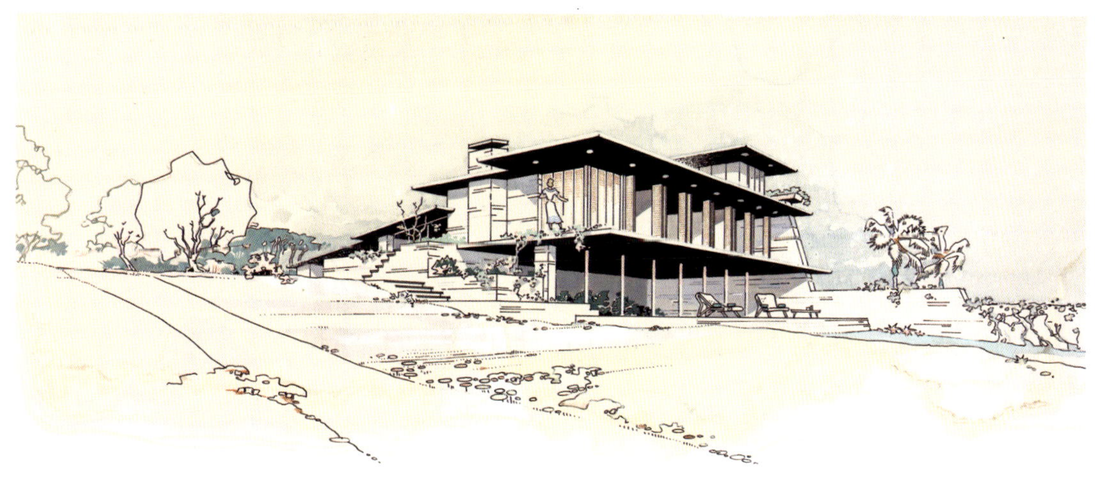

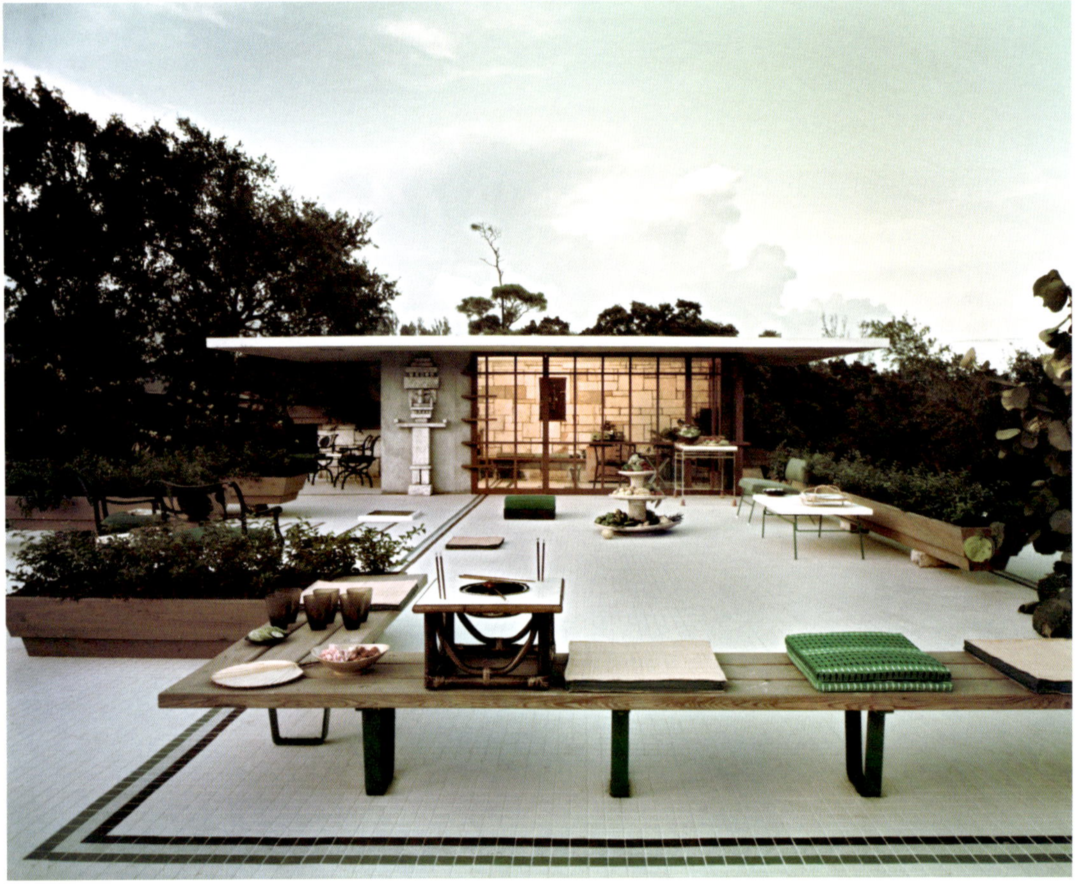

Parker Residence (Pace Setter 1954), Coconut Grove, 1952
Roof terrace and home office
Photograph © Ezra Stoller/ESTO
ESTO

Parker Residence (Pace Setter 1954), Coconut Grove, 1952
Chimney and terrace
Photograph © Ezra Stoller/ESTO
ESTO

Parker Residence (Pace Setter 1954), Coconut Grove, 1952
Parti drawing
Ink on paper, 8" x 4"
George A. Smathers Libraries, University of Florida

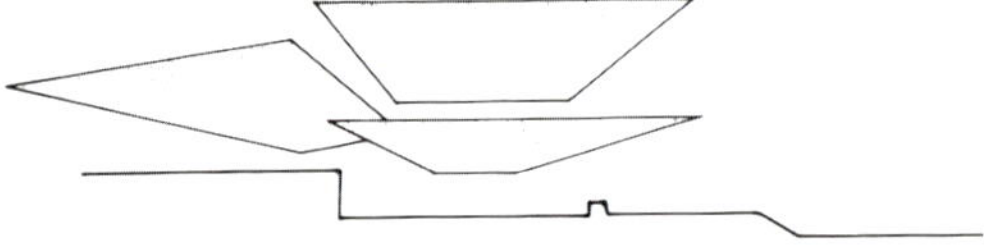

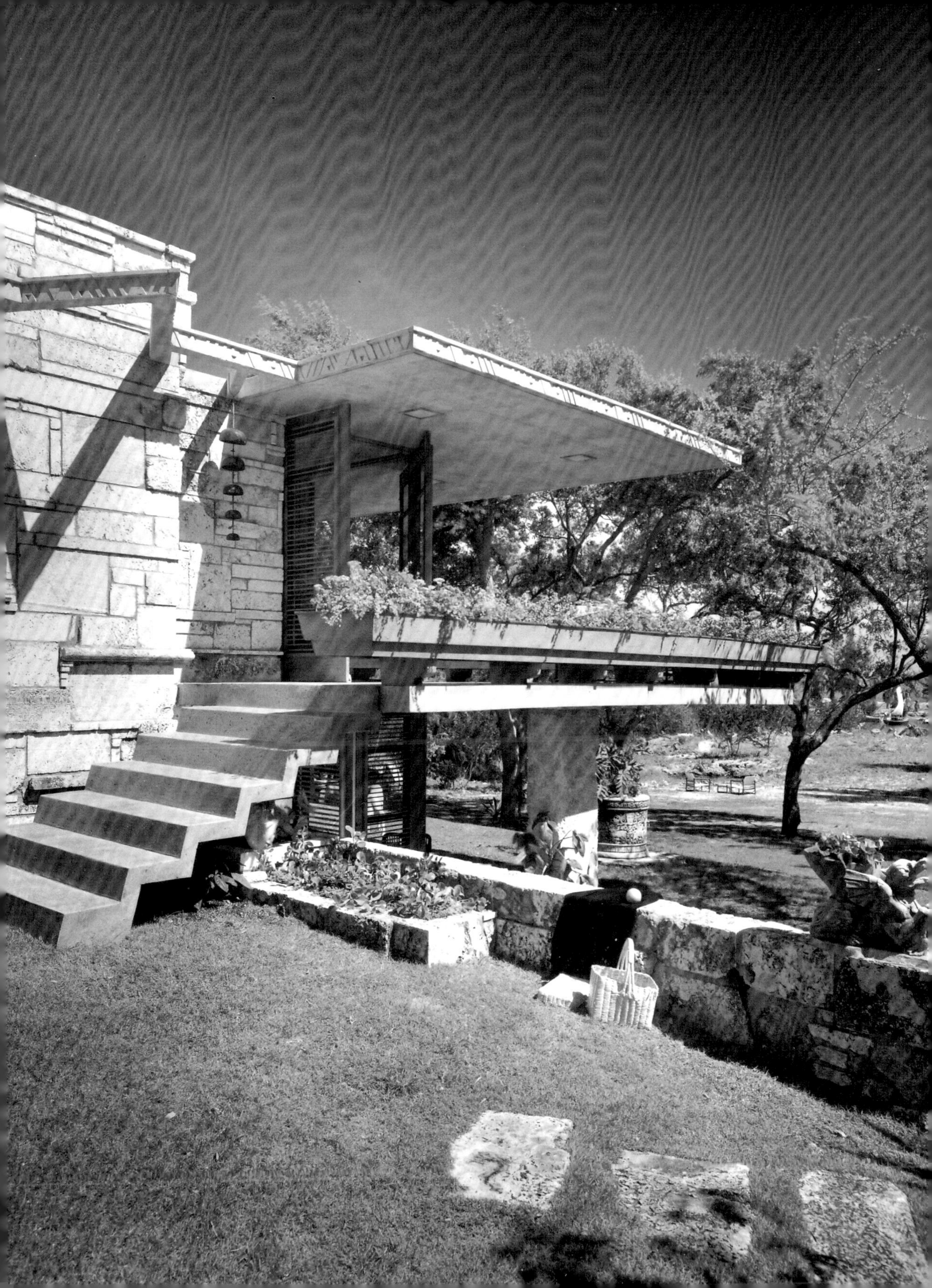

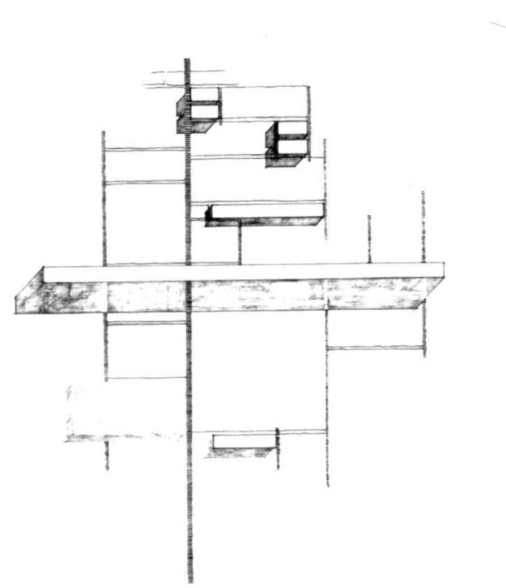

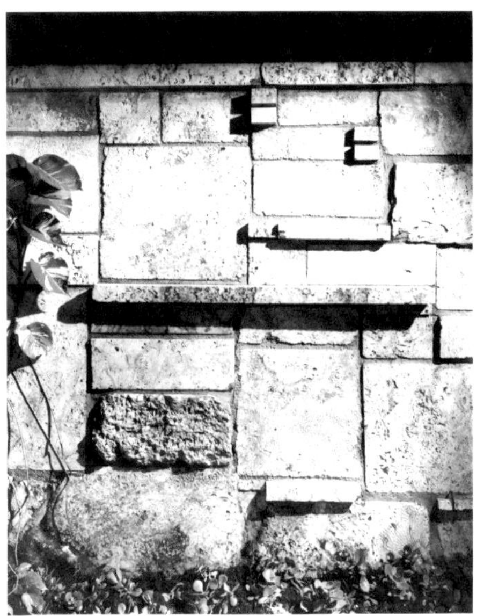

Stone joining based on Butterick sewing pattern no. 1289564, undated
Pencil on paper, 8" x 9"
George A. Smathers Libraries, University of Florida

Stone wall at Parker Residence, ca. 1952
B&W vintage photograph, 8" x 10"
Photograph © Ezra Stoller/ESTO
Courtesy of Randolph C. Henning

Alfred Browning Parker building the Parker Residence, ca. 1952
Photograph © Ezra Stoller/ESTO
ESTO

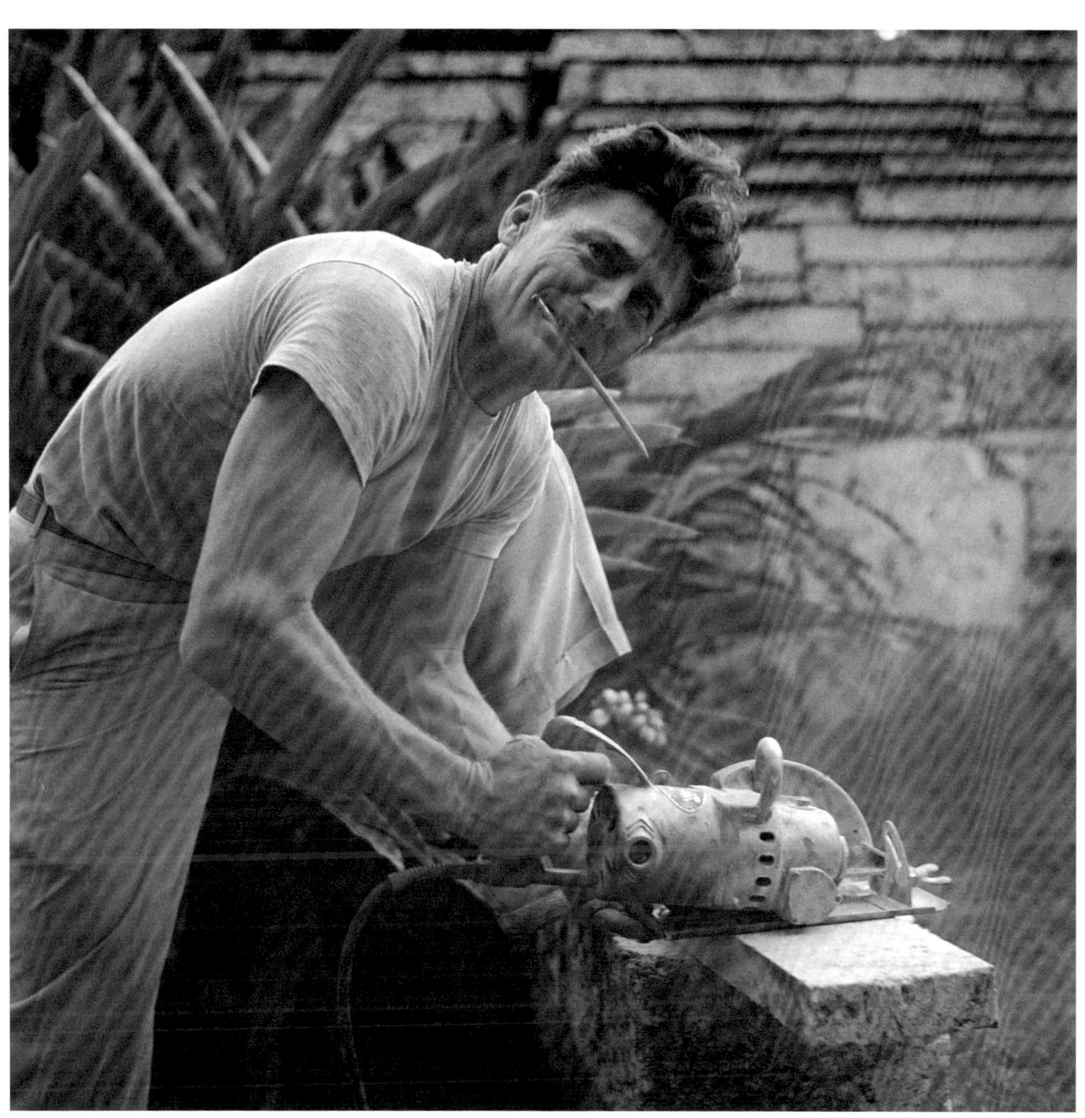

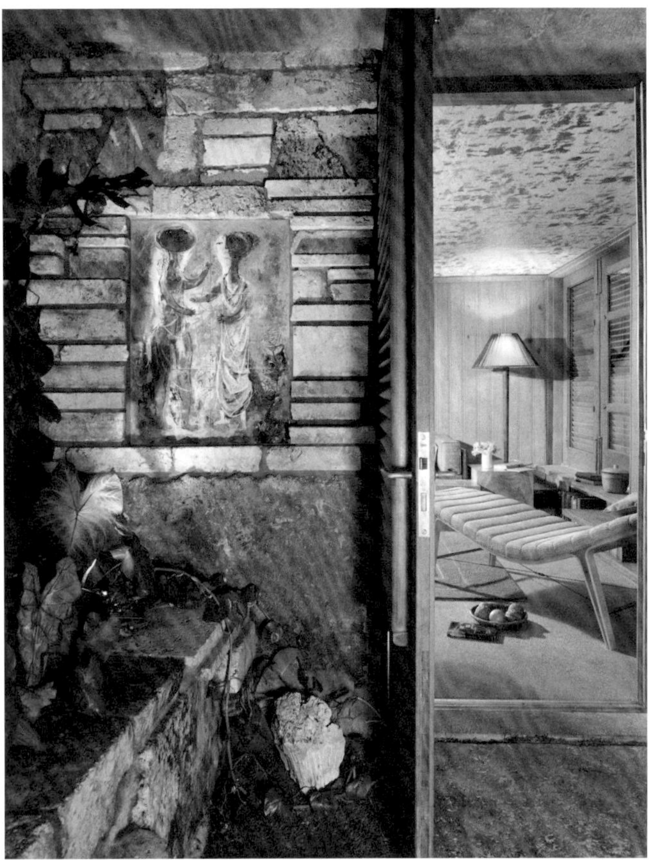

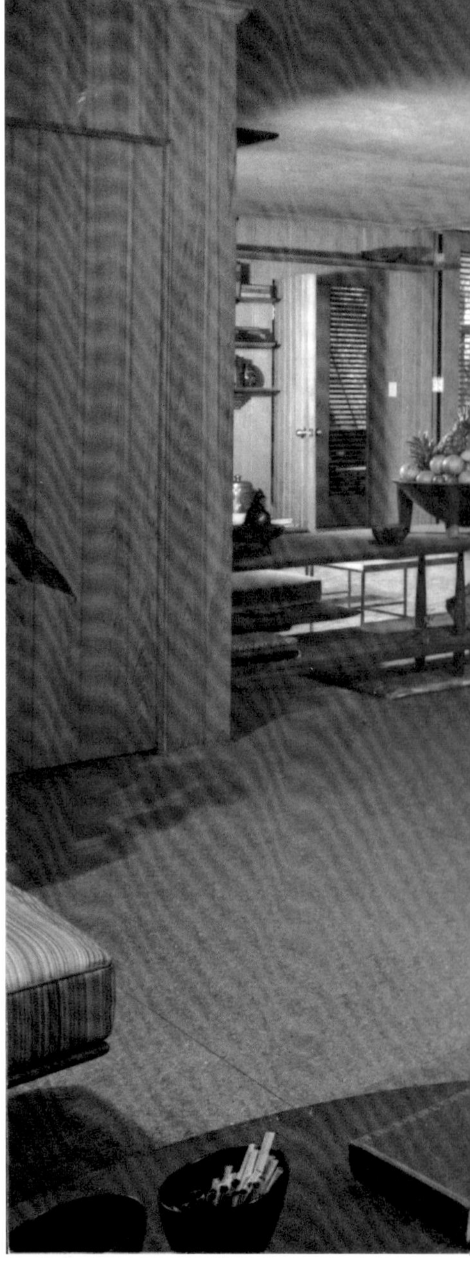

Parker Residence (Pace Setter 1954), Coconut Grove, 1952
Ground floor bedroom
Photograph © Ezra Stoller/ESTO
ESTO

Parker Residence (Pace Setter 1954), Coconut Grove, 1952
Living room
Photograph © Ezra Stoller/ESTO
ESTO

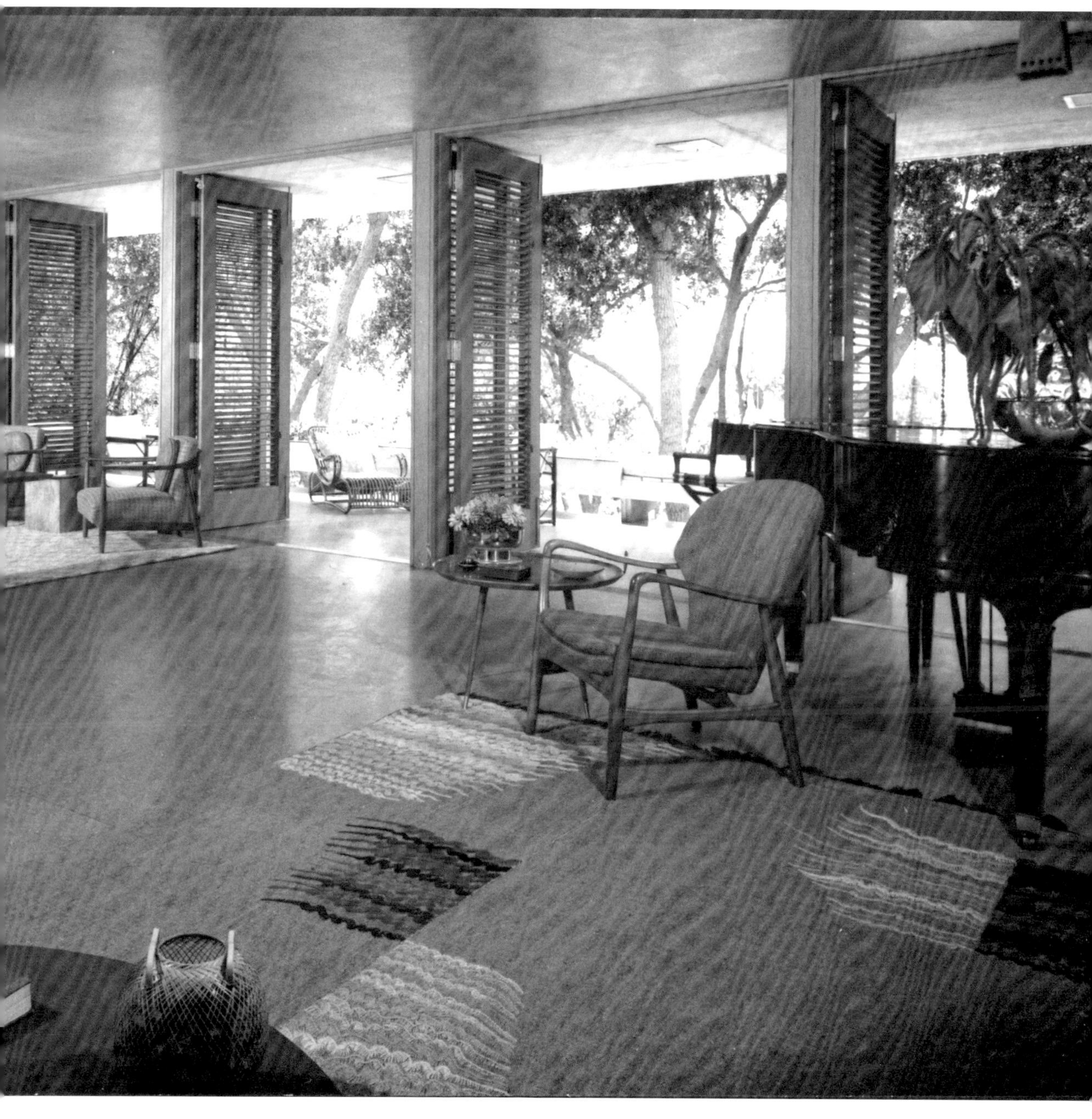

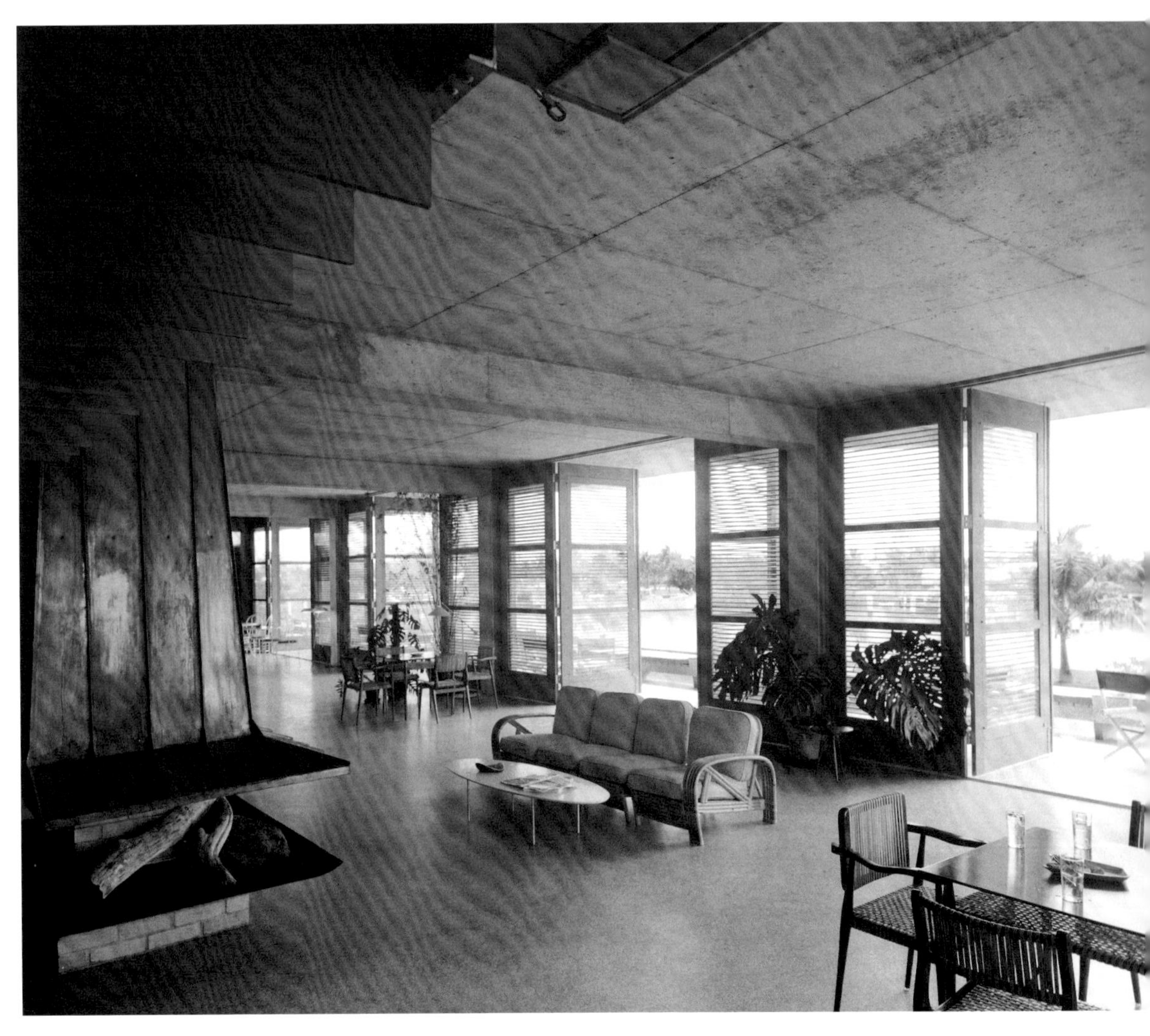

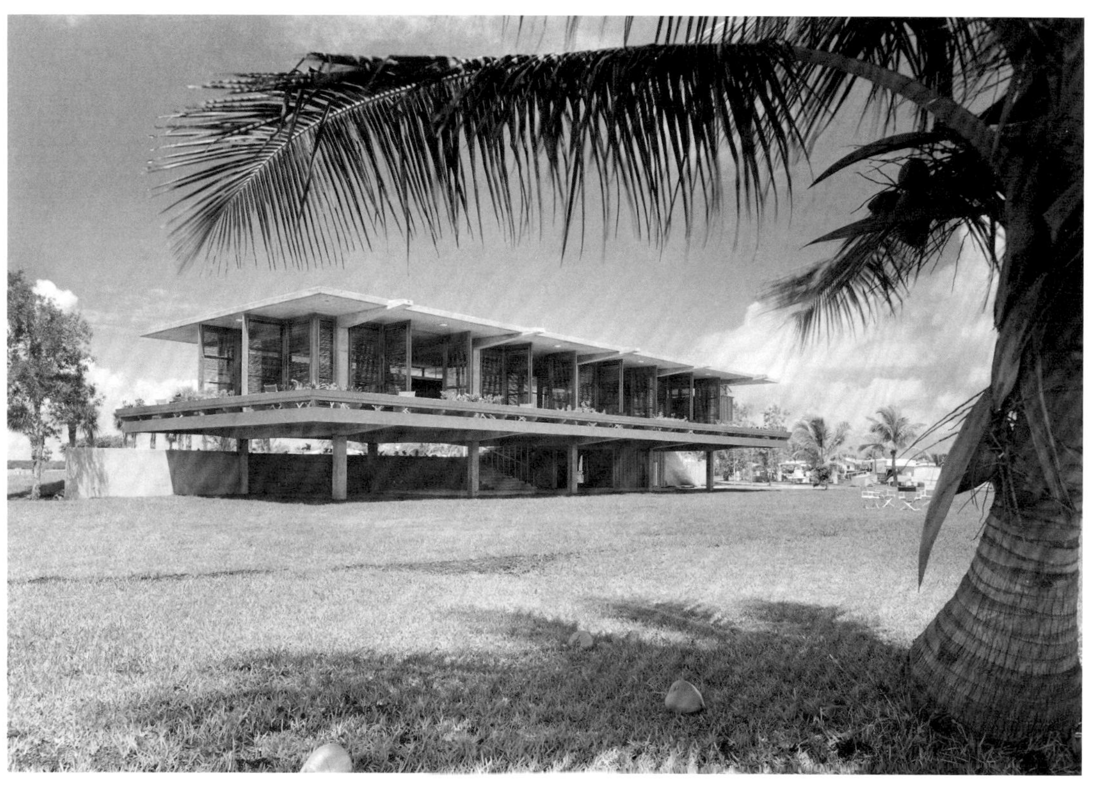

Bal Harbour Club, Bal Harbour, 1952
Club interior
B&W vintage photograph, 8" x 10"
Photograph © Ezra Stoller/ESTO
Courtesy of Randolph C. Henning

Bal Harbour Club, Bal Harbour, 1952
B&W vintage photograph, 8" x 10"
Photograph © Ezra Stoller/ESTO
Courtesy of Randolph C. Henning

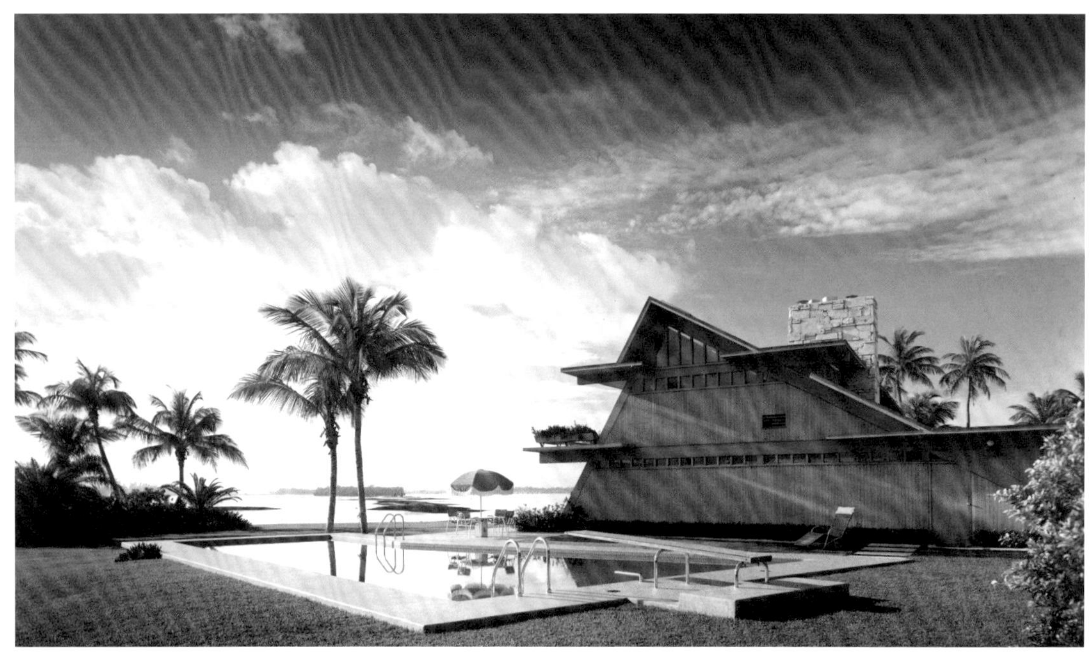

Mass Residence, Palm Beach, 1954
B&W vintage photograph, 14" x 11 ¼"
Photograph © Ezra Stoller/ESTO
George A. Smathers Libraries, University of Florida

Mass Residence, Palm Beach, 1954
Living area
Photograph © Ezra Stoller/ESTO
ESTO

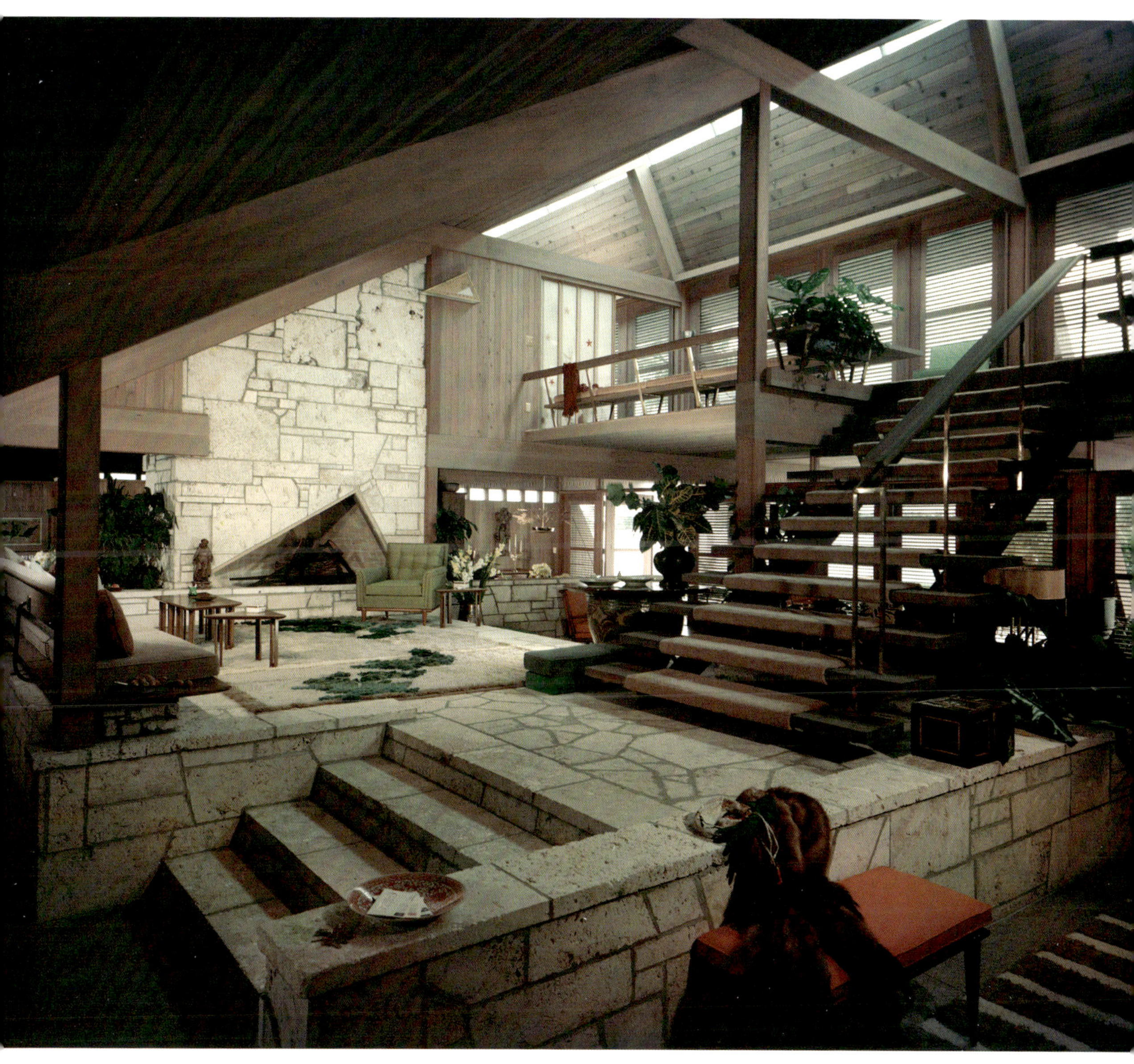

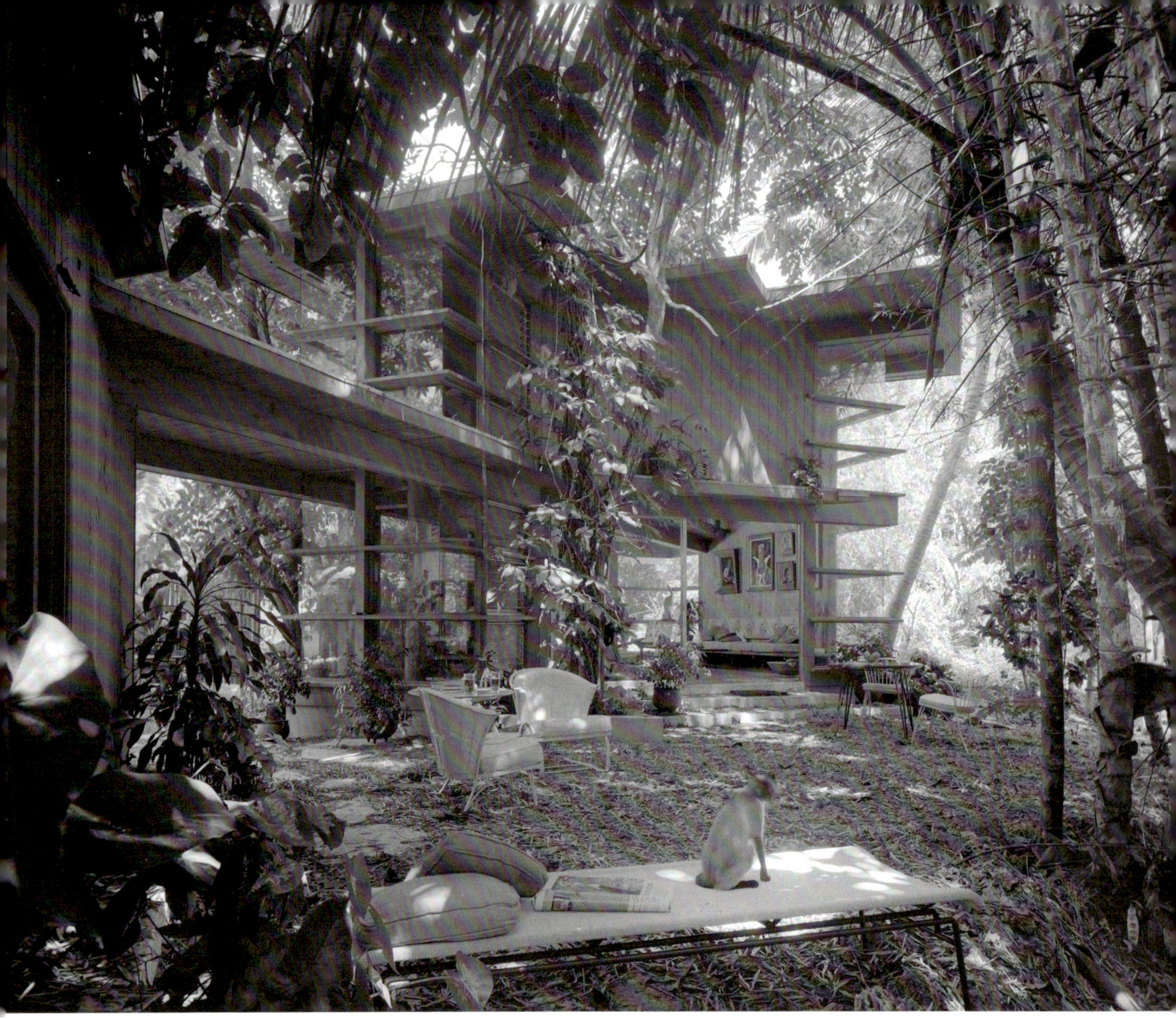

Gayer Residence, Coconut Grove, 1953
Garden patio
Photograph © Ezra Stoller/ESTO
ESTO

Gayer Residence, Coconut Grove, 1953
Upholstery stamp
Mahogany, 10” x 10”
Patrick and Jodi Farrell

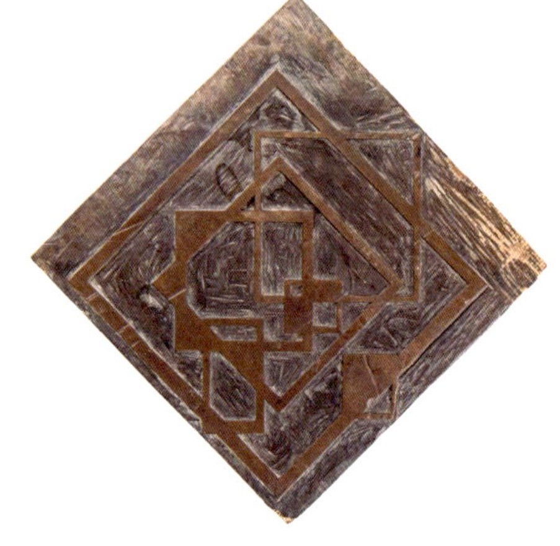

Gayer Residence, Coconut Grove, 1953
Living area
Photograph © Ezra Stoller/ESTO
ESTO

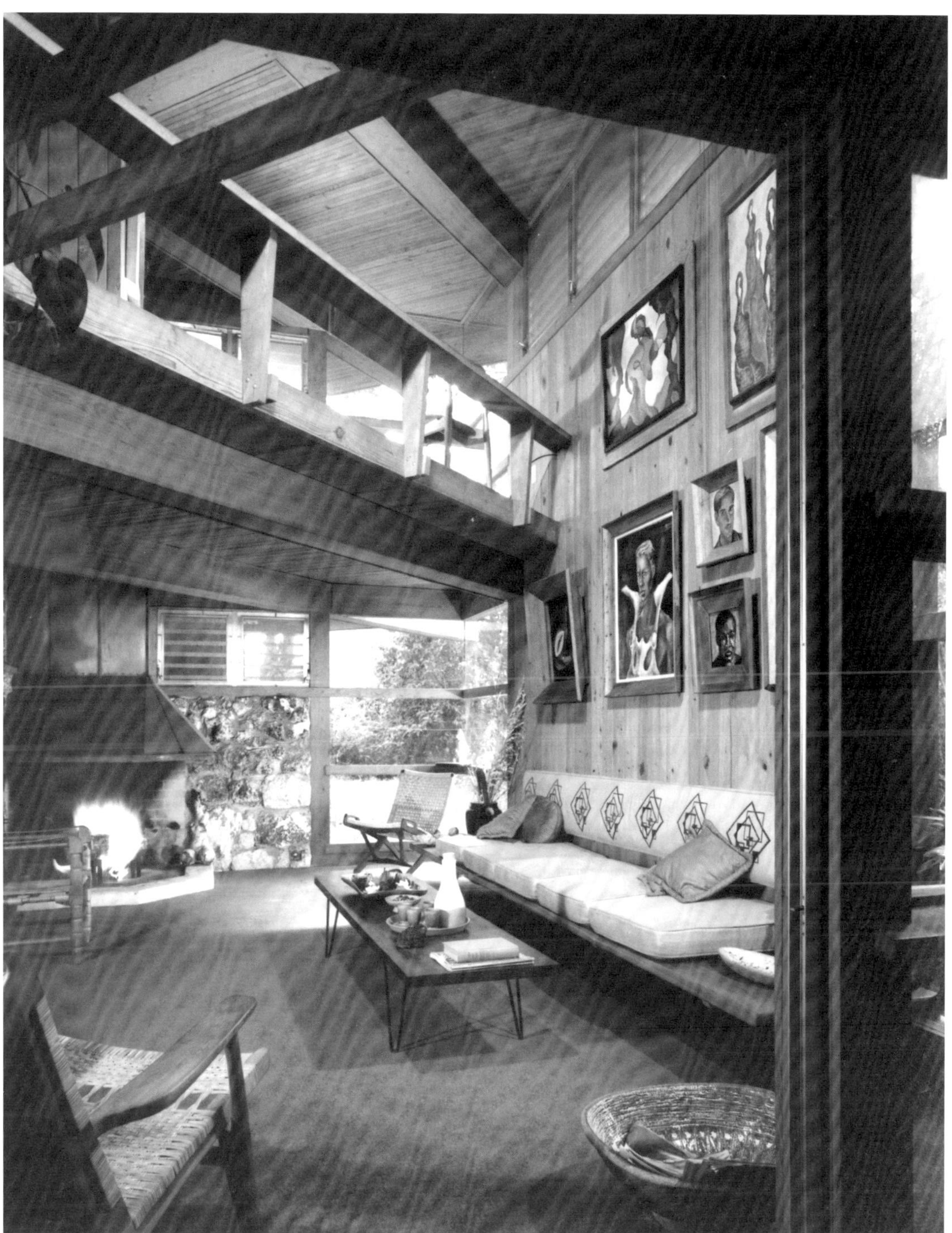

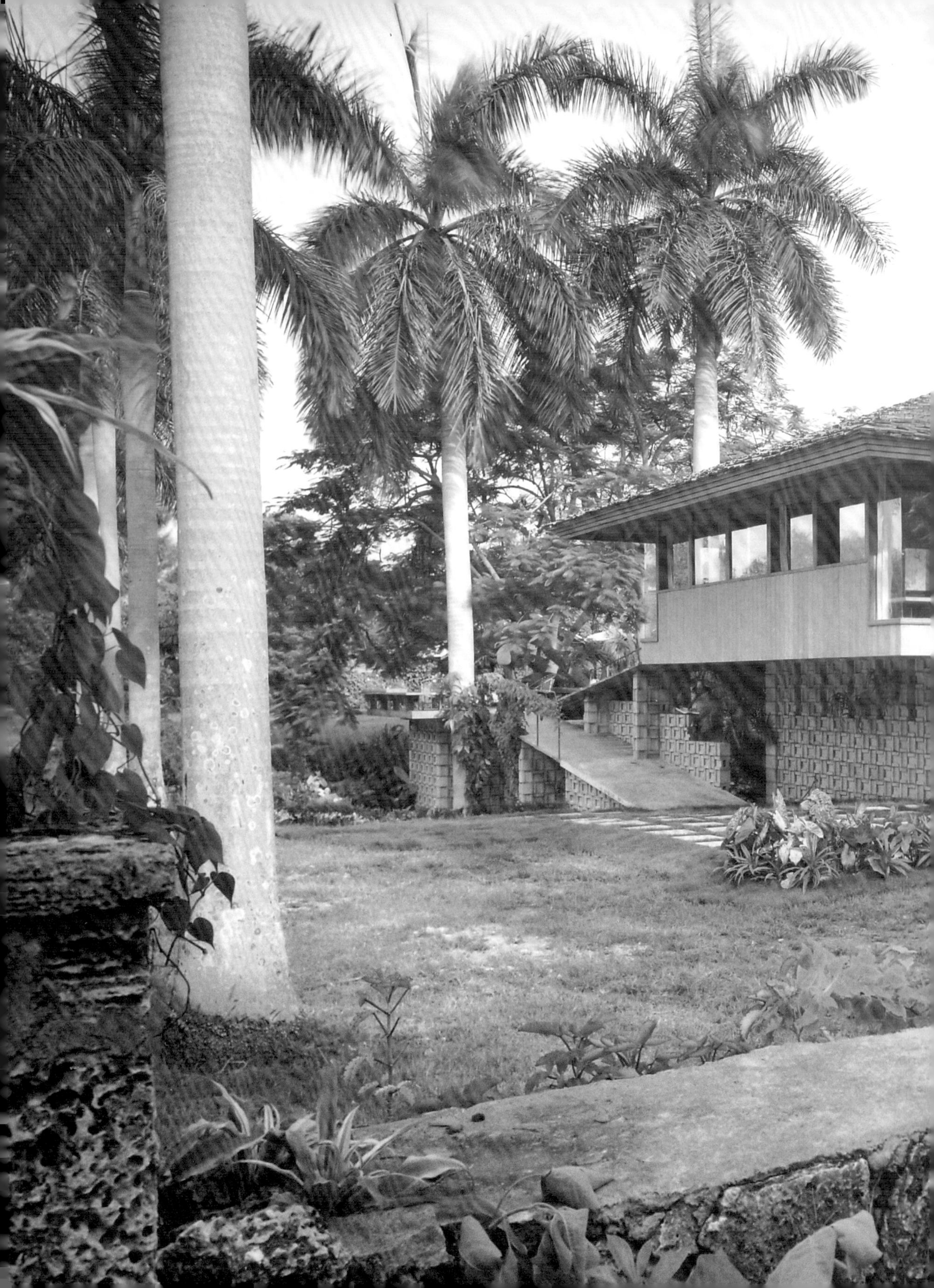

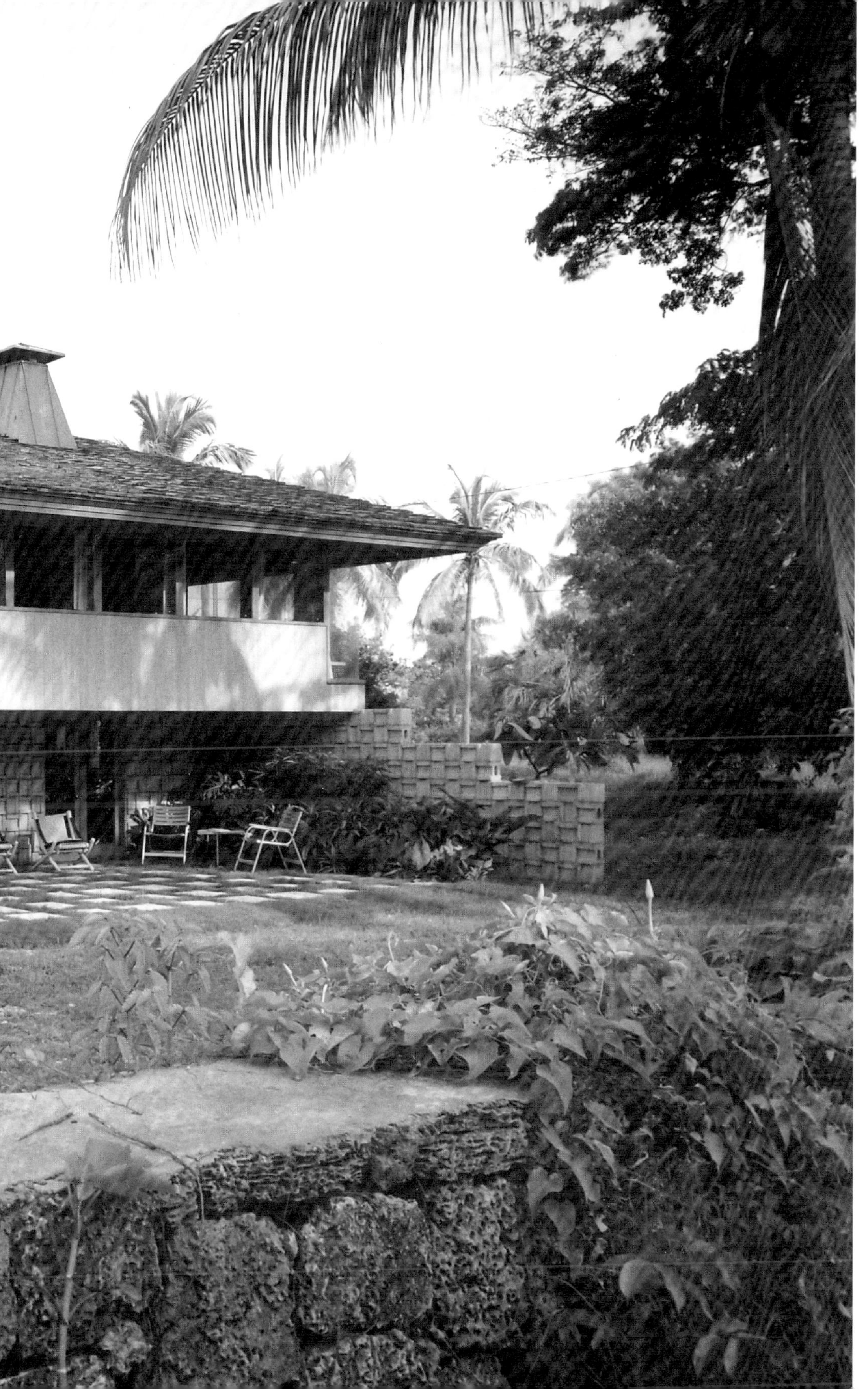

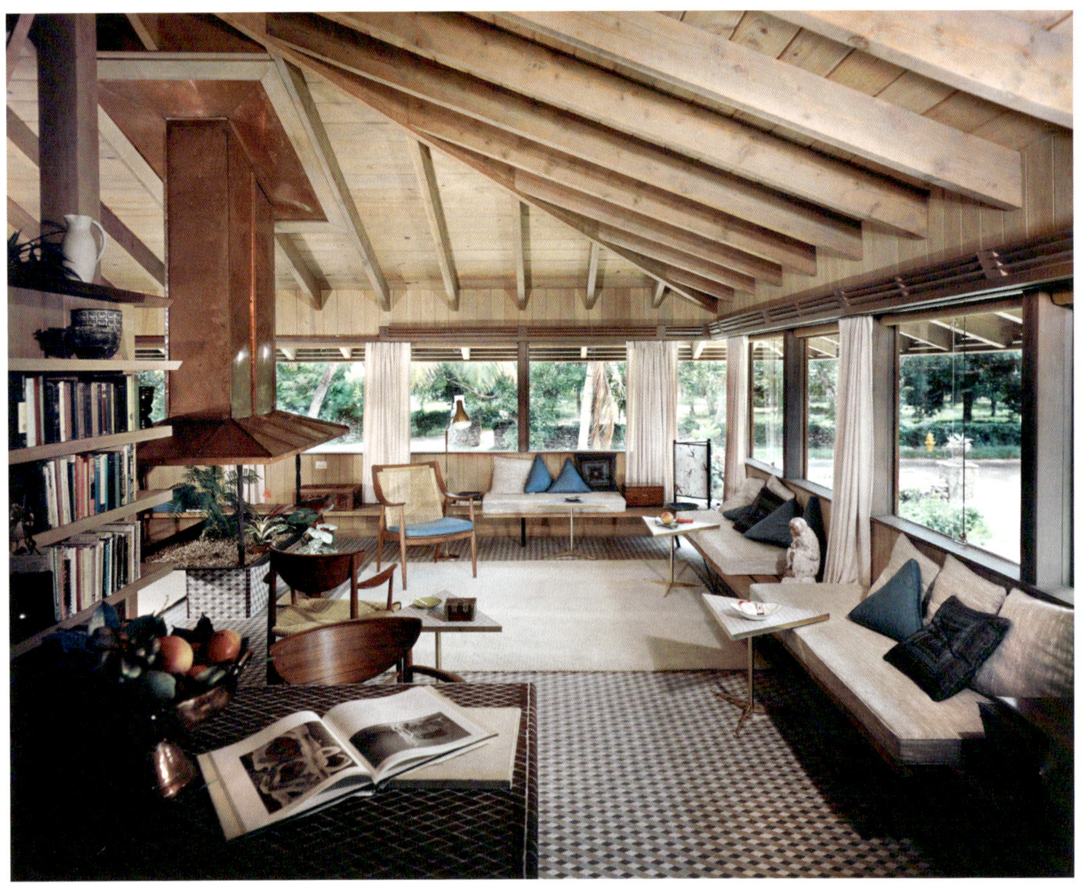

Previous page: Ewing Residence, Coconut Grove, 1955
Photograph © Ezra Stoller/ESTO
ESTO

Ewing Residence, Coconut Grove, 1955
Living area
Photograph © Ezra Stoller/ESTO
ESTO

Ewing Residence, Coconut Grove, 1955
Corner of living area
Photograph © Ezra Stoller/ESTO
ESTO

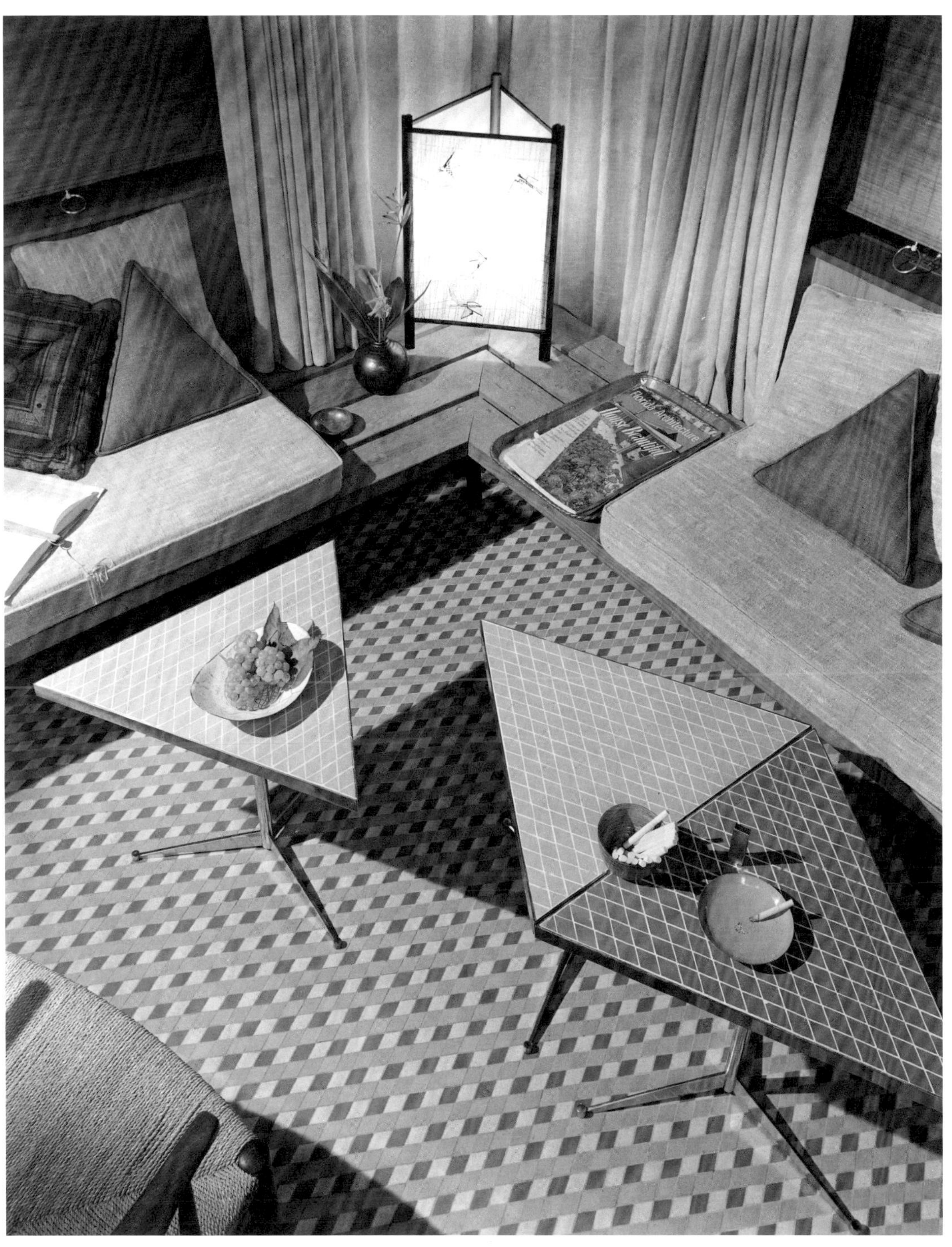
Florida Architecture
House Beautiful

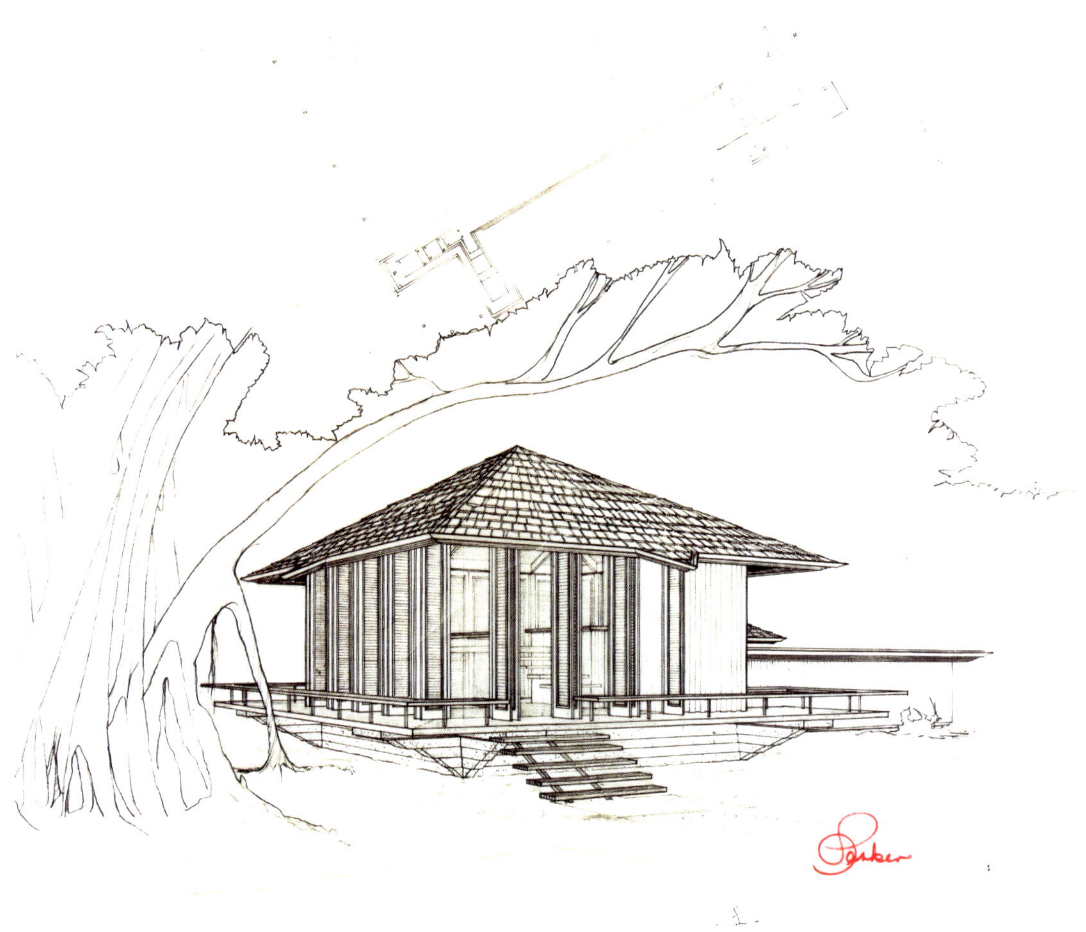

Jewel Parker Residence, Coconut Grove, 1957
Perspective view of main pavilion
Pencil on yellow trace paper, 18" x 15"
Courtesy of Randolph C. Henning

Jewel Parker Residence, Coconut Grove, 1957
Living area
Photograph © Ezra Stoller/ESTO
ESTO

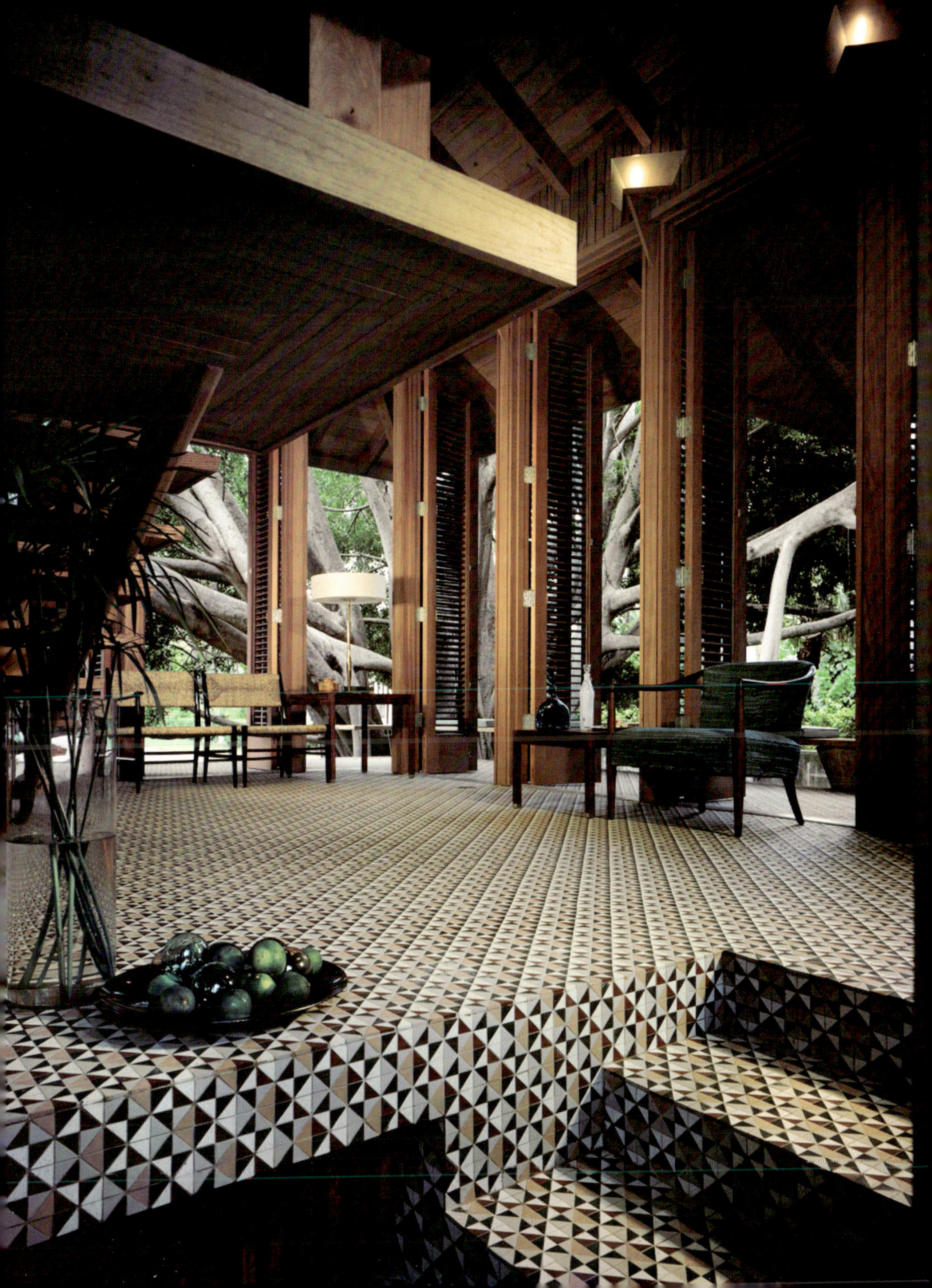

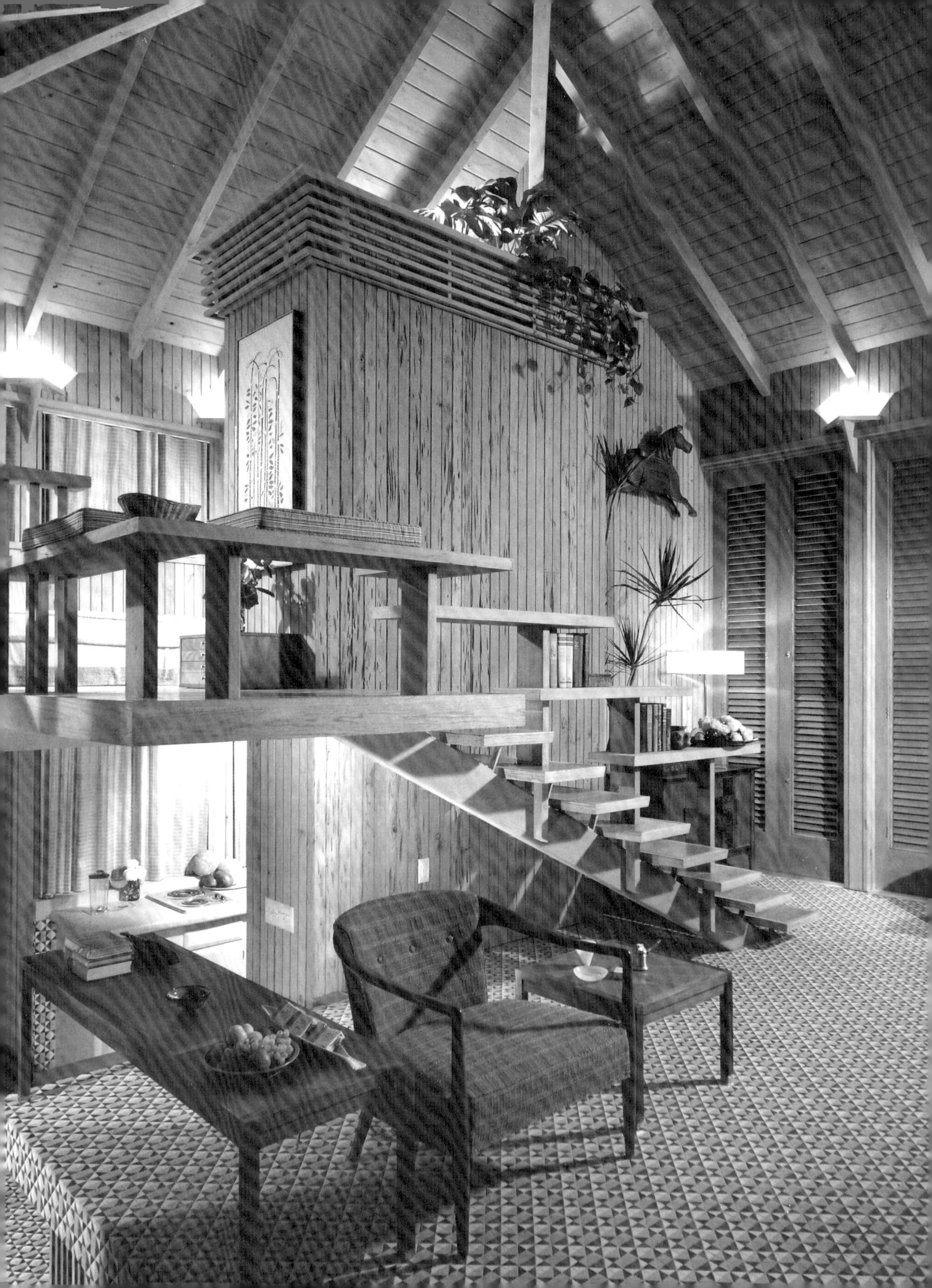

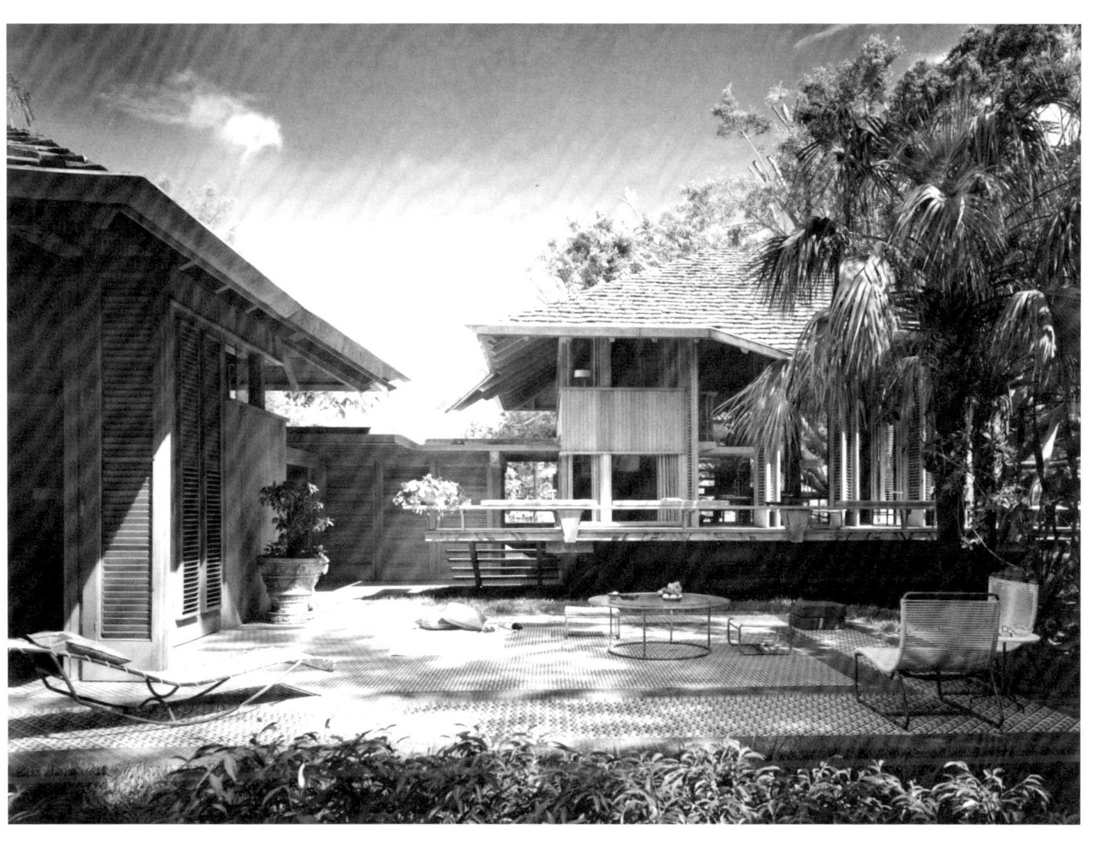

Jewel Parker Residence, Coconut Grove, 1957
Living area with stair wrapping core
Photograph © Ezra Stoller/ESTO
ESTO

Jewel Parker Residence, Coconut Grove, 1957
Photograph © Ezra Stoller/ESTO
ESTO

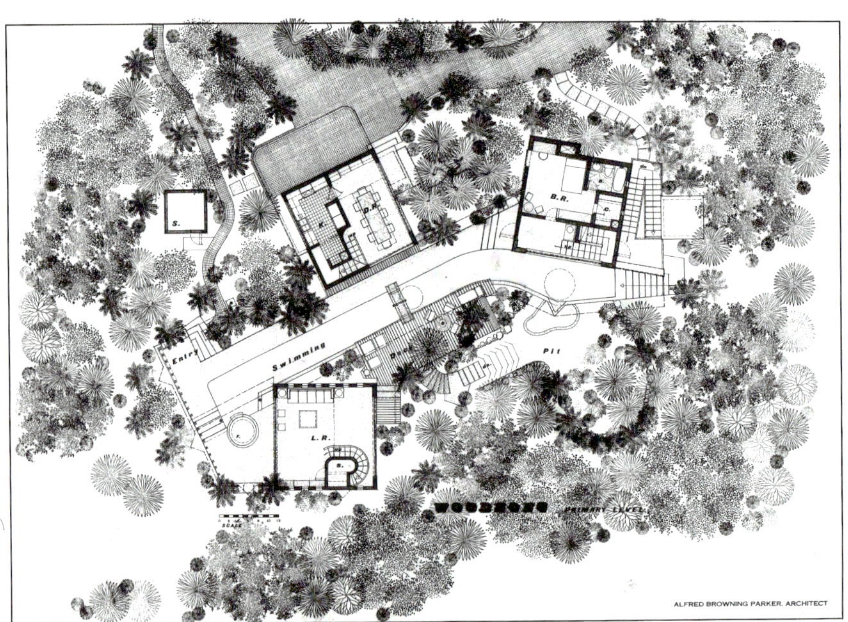

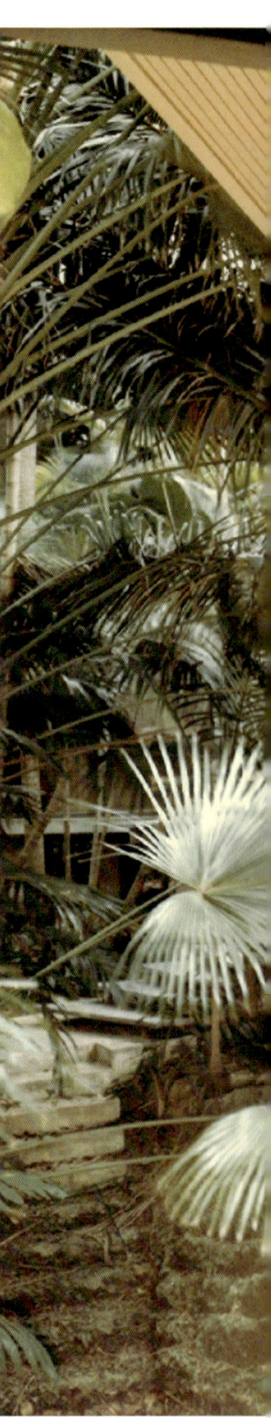

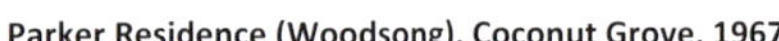

Parker Residence (Woodsong), Coconut Grove, 1967
Ground floor plan
Ink and pencil on paper, 42" x 30"
George A. Smathers Libraries, University of Florida

Parker Residence (Woodsong), Coconut Grove, 1967
Color vintage photograph, 8" x 10"
Photograph © Bo Parker
Courtesy of Randolph C. Henning

Next page: Friedman Residence (Mini-Pace Setter), Coconut Grove, 1953
Photograph © Ezra Stoller/ESTO
ESTO

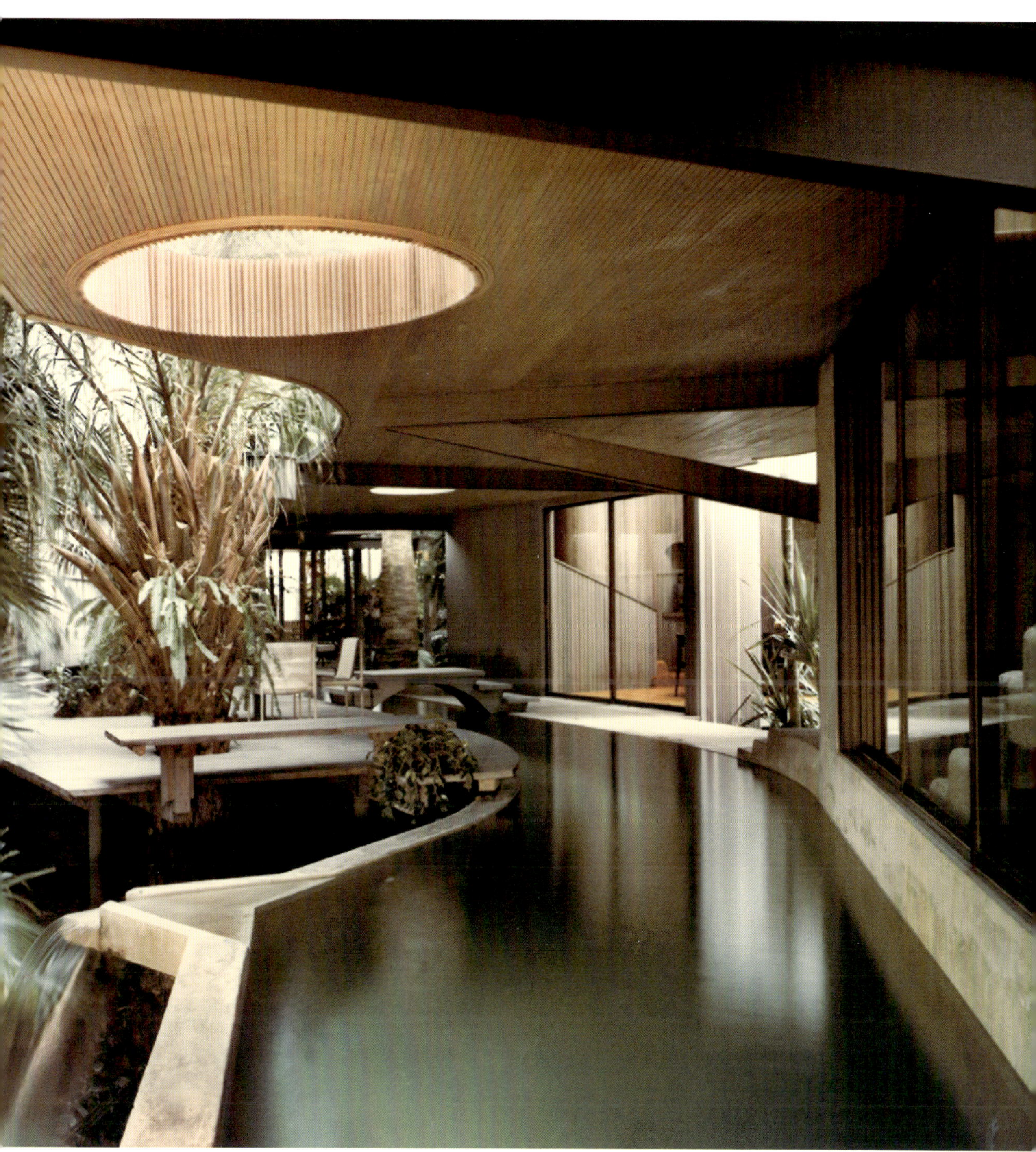

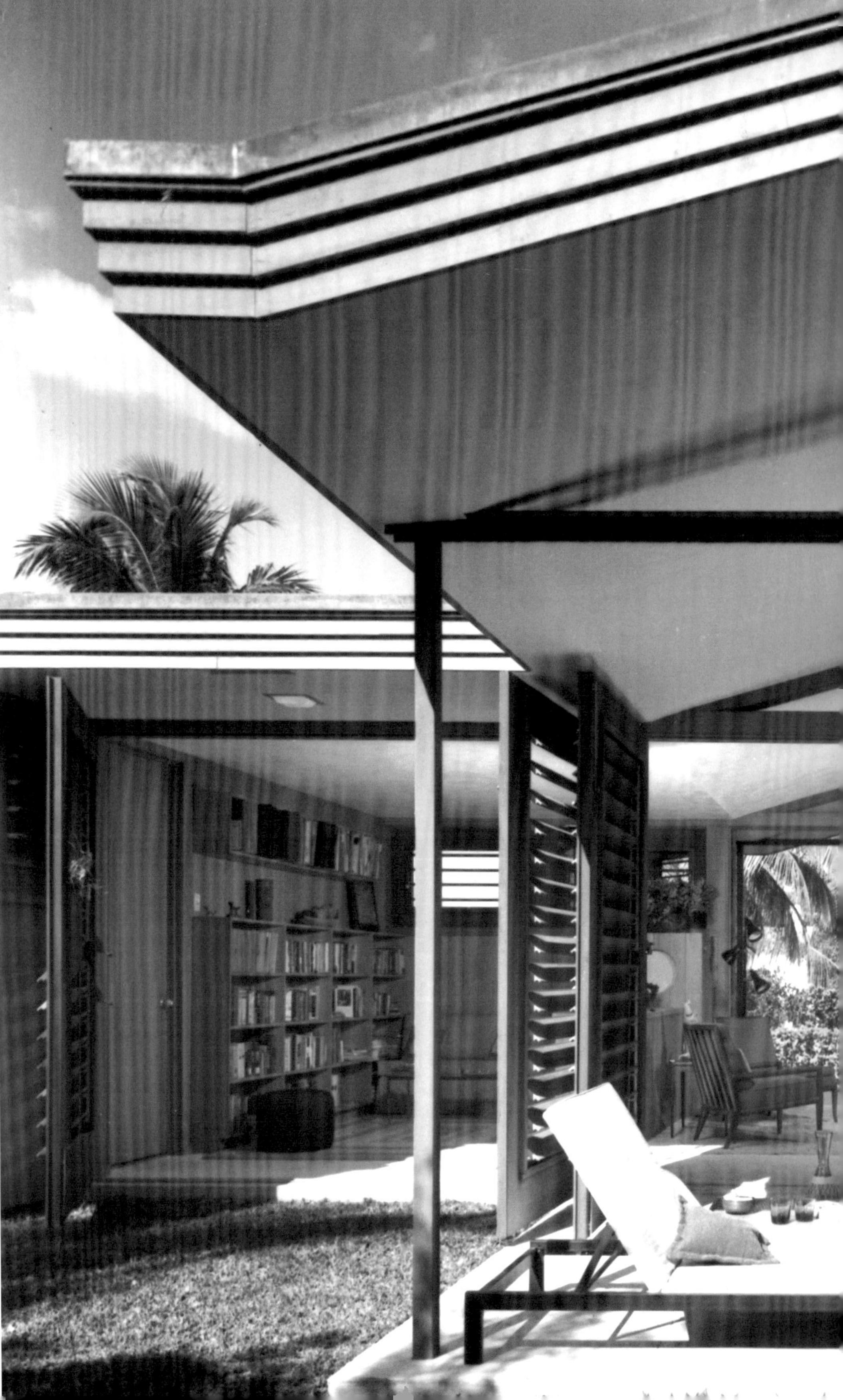

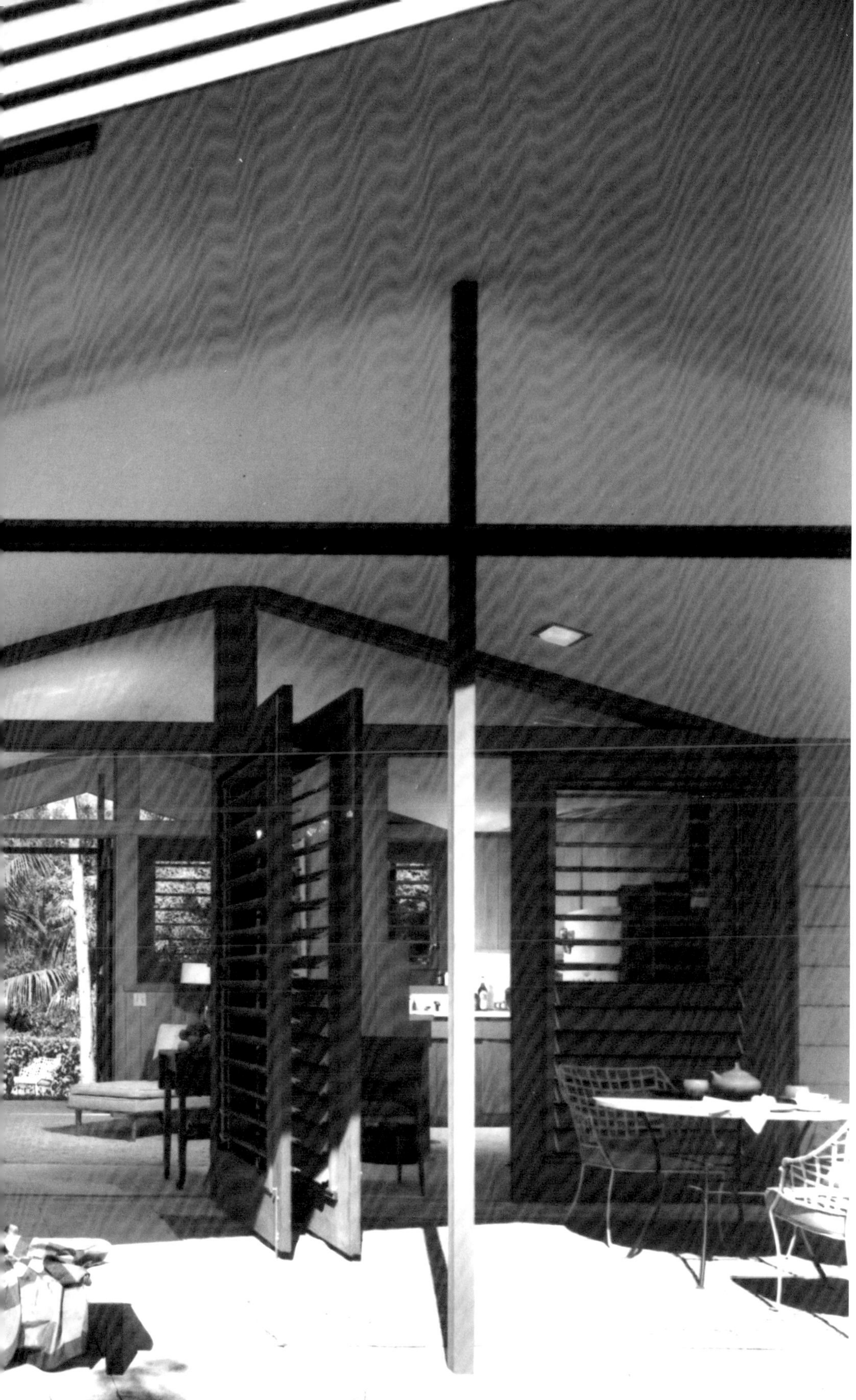

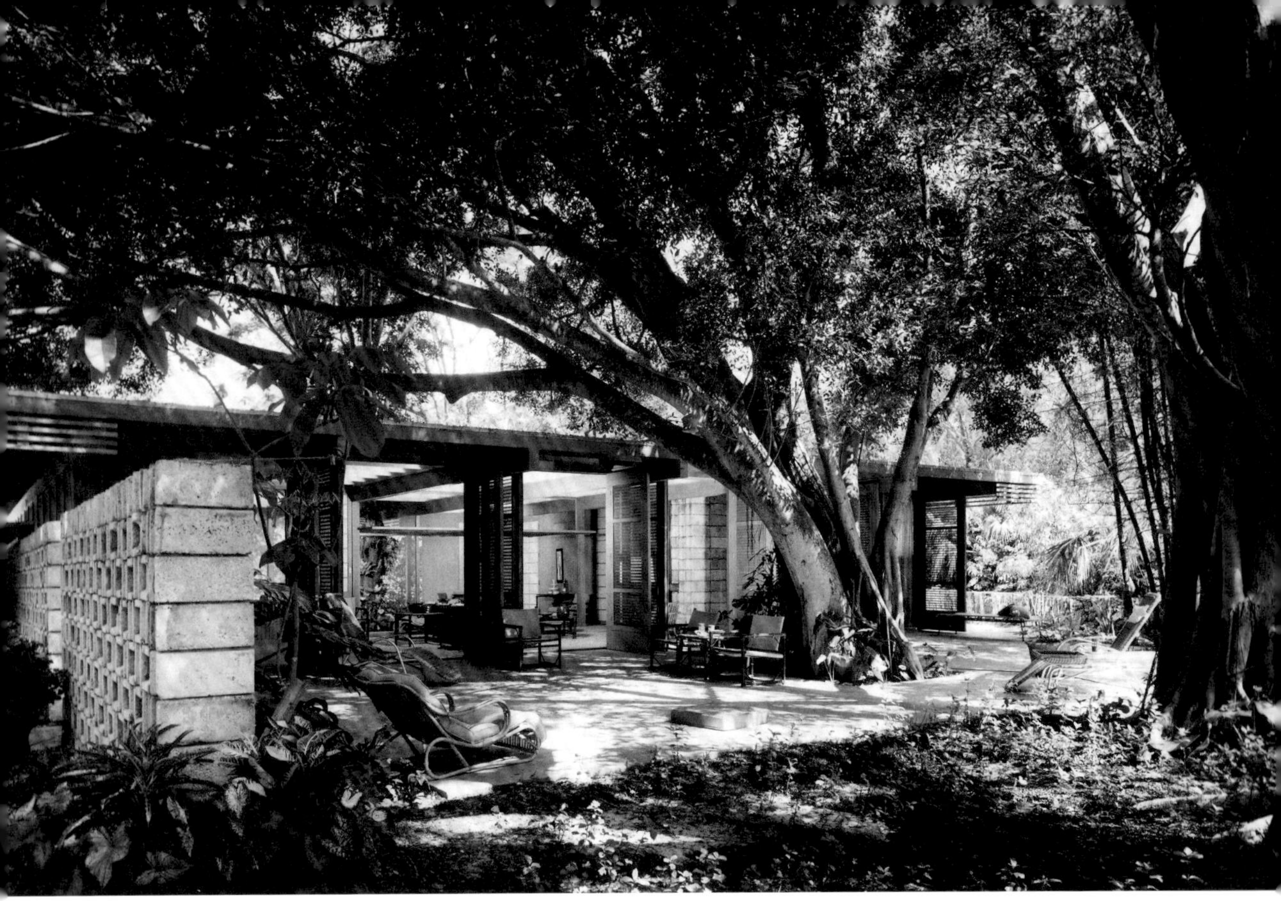

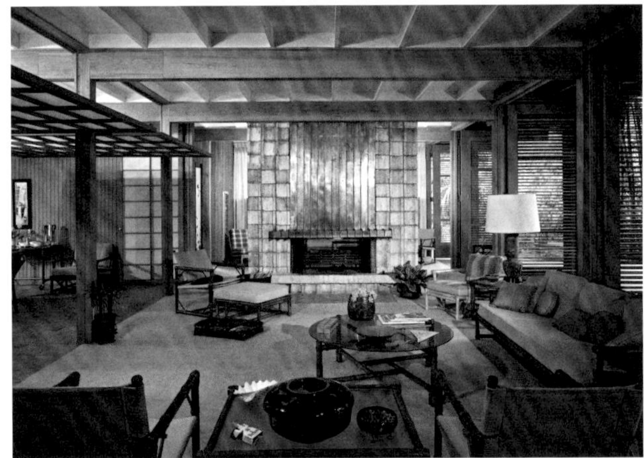

Marko Residence, Coconut Grove, 1955
B&W vintage photograph, 10" x 8"
Photograph © Ezra Stoller/ESTO
Courtesy of Randolph C. Henning

Marko Residence, Coconut Grove, 1955
Living room
Photograph © Ezra Stoller/ESTO
ESTO

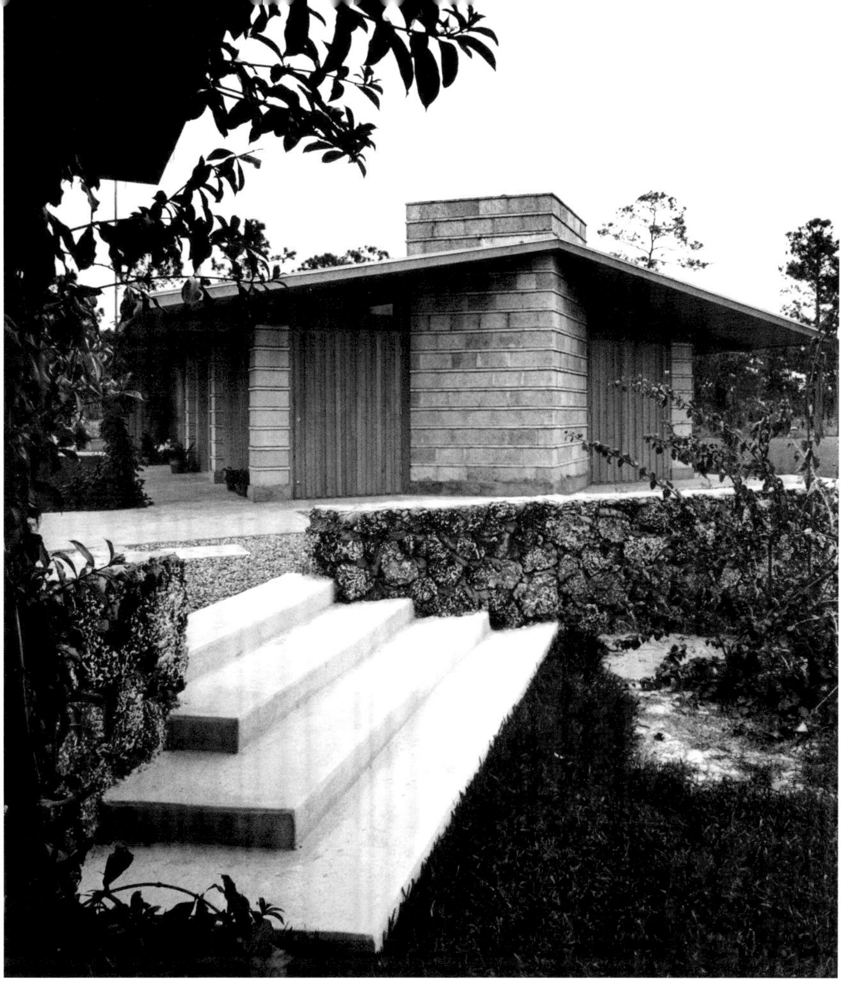

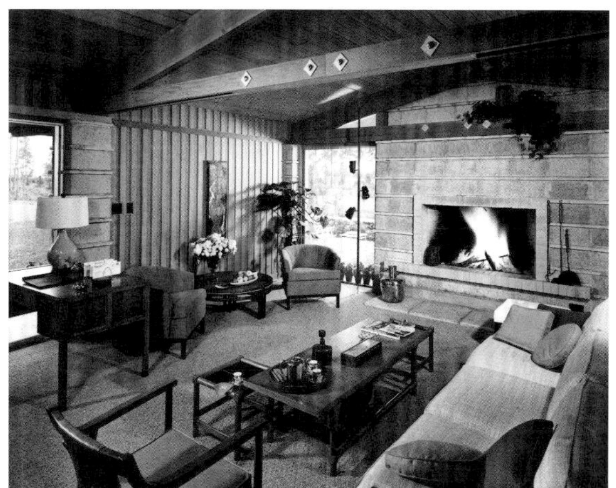

Kitchens Residence, Miami-Dade County, 1956
B&W vintage photograph, 10" x 8"
Photograph © Ezra Stoller/ESTO
Courtesy of Randolph C. Henning

Kitchens Residence, Miami-Dade County, 1956
Living area
B&W vintage photograph, 10" x 8"
Photograph © Ezra Stoller/ESTO
Courtesy of Randolph C. Henning

Next page: Good Residence, Sea Ranch Lakes, 1960
Living area
Photograph © Ezra Stoller/ESTO
ESTO

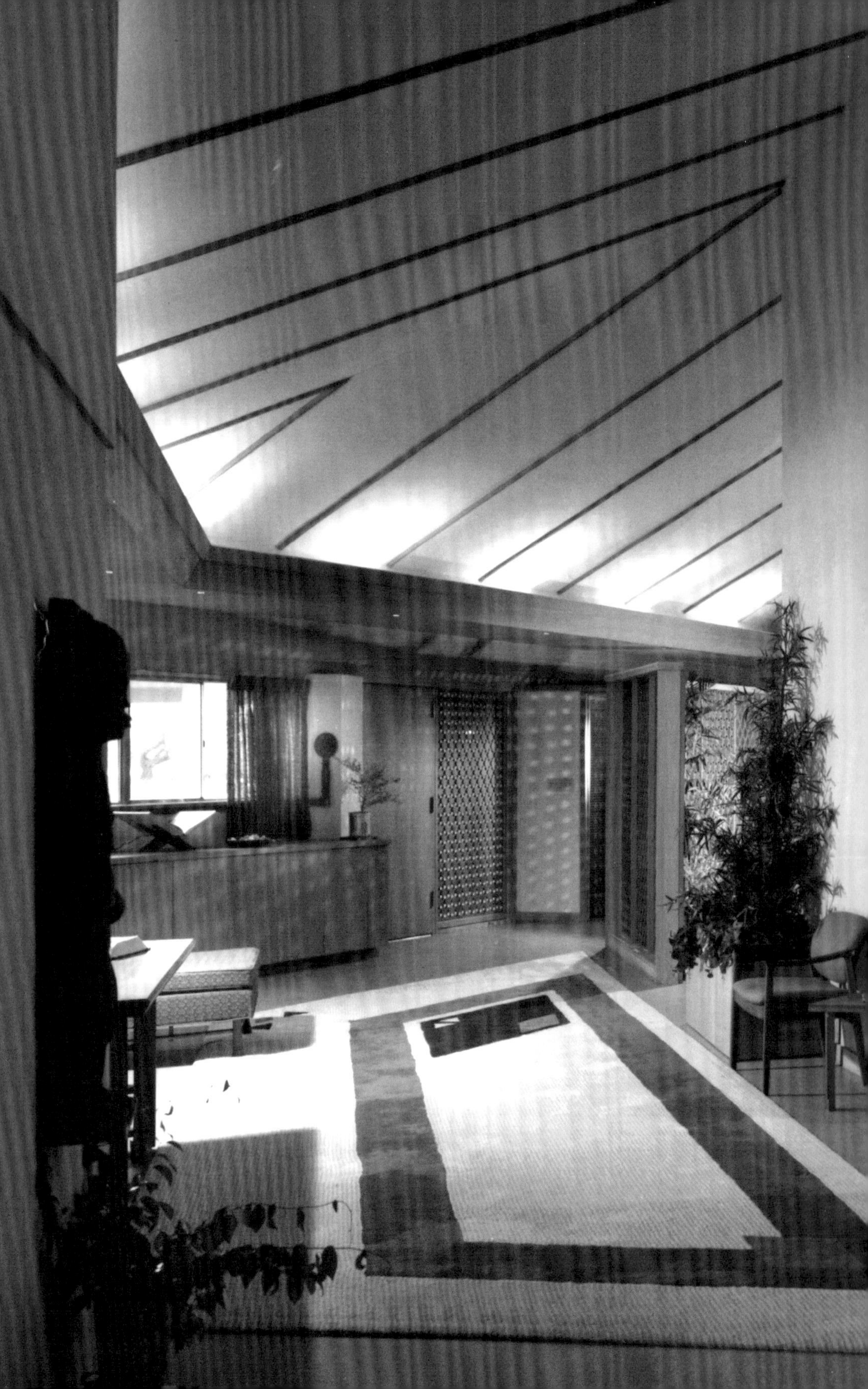

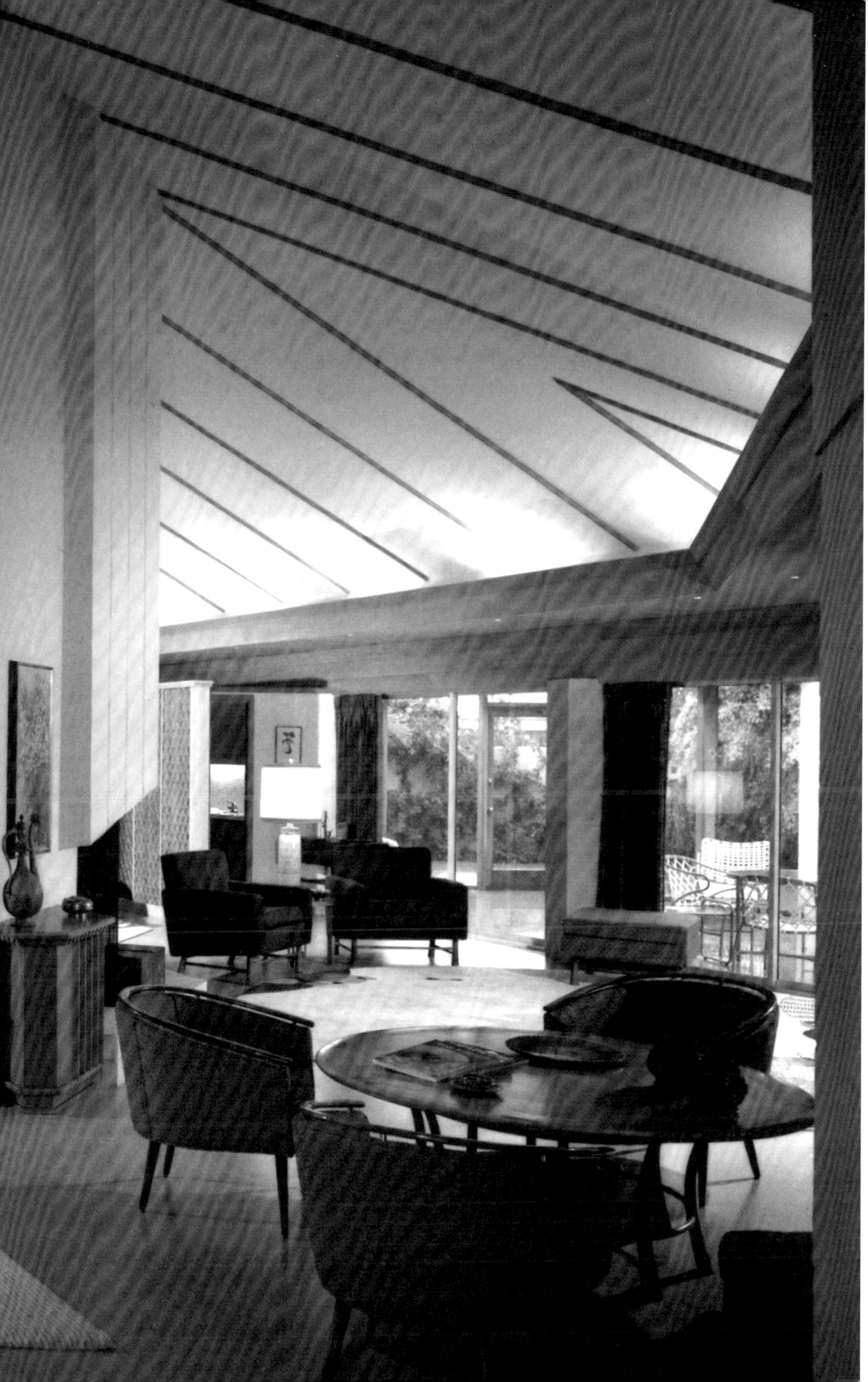

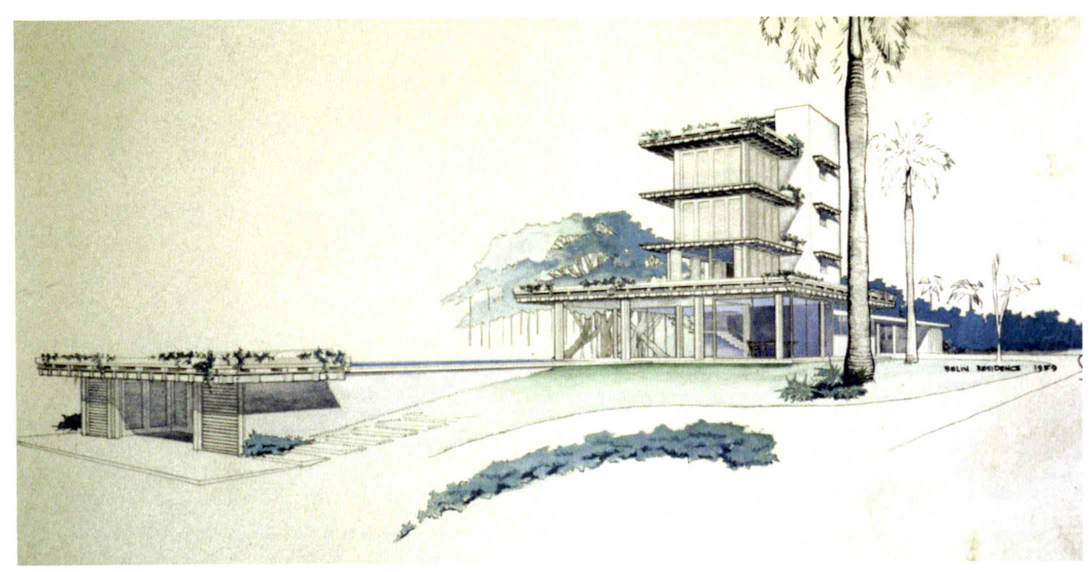

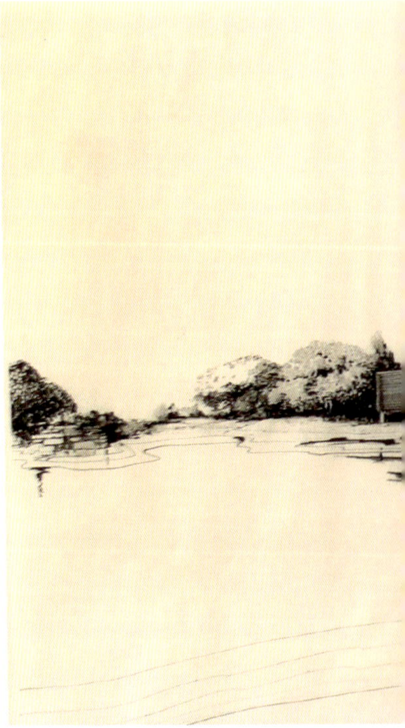

Belin Residence, Coconut Grove, 1959 (unbuilt)
Perspective rendering
Ink and watercolor on board, 41" x 18"
George A. Smathers Libraries, University of Florida

Crane Residence, Rachel Cove, Marathon Shores, 1972 (unbuilt)
Perspective rendering
Ink on vellum, signed John G. Adams, 41" x 16"
Courtesy of Randolph C. Henning

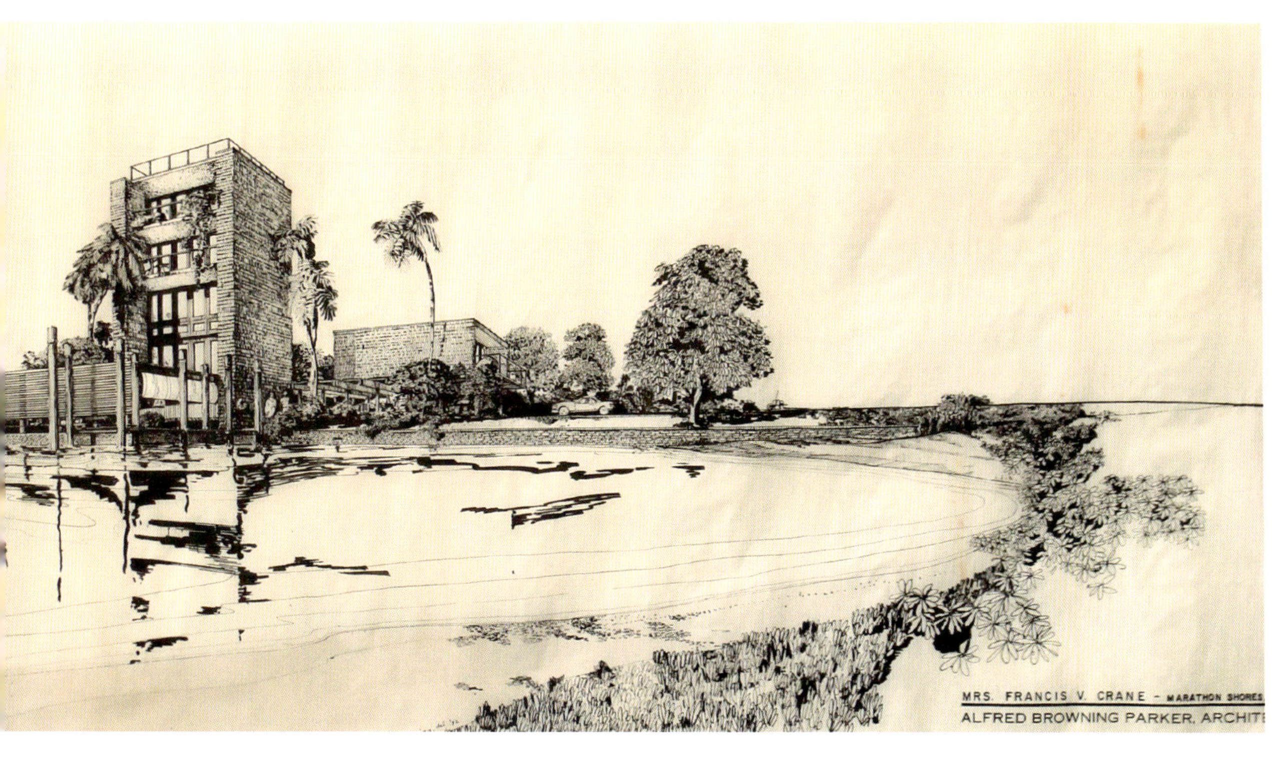
MRS. FRANCIS V. CRANE - MARATHON SHORES
ALFRED BROWNING PARKER, ARCHIT

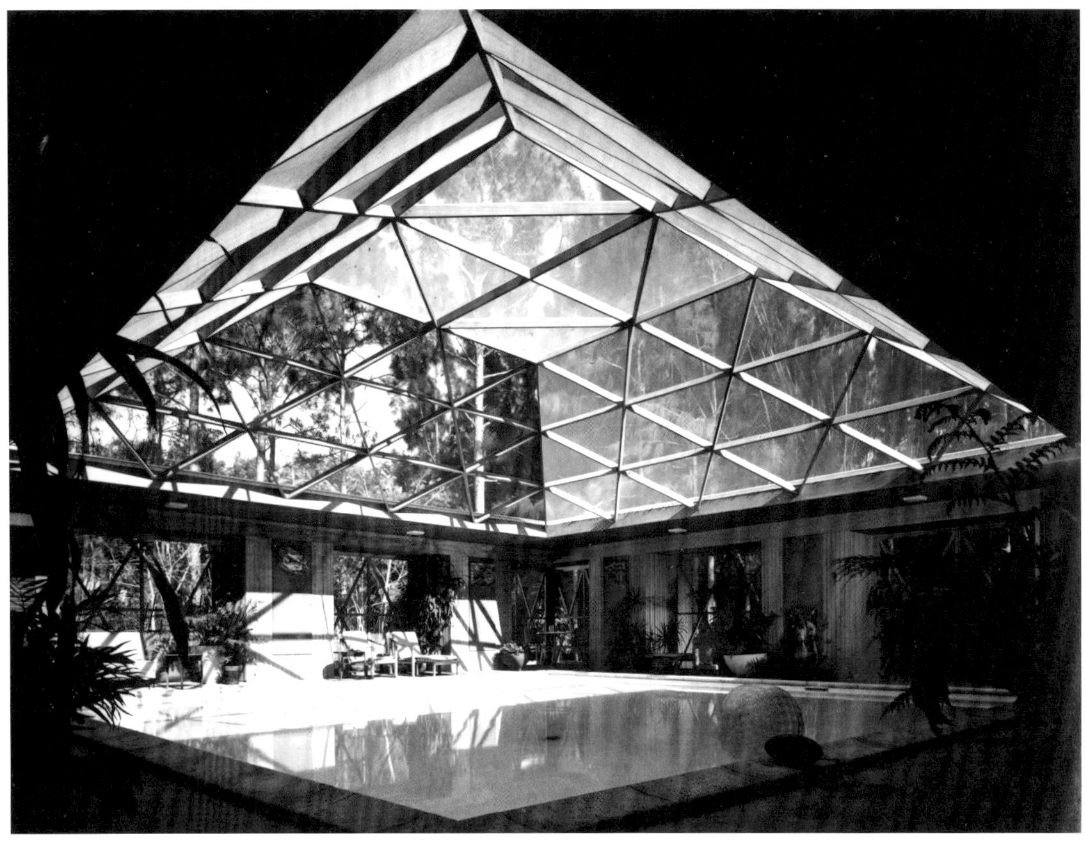

Miller Residence (Pace Setter 1959), Coconut Grove, 1957
Screened patio
Photograph © Ezra Stoller/ESTO
ESTO

Minimum Maintenance House for *Popular Mechanics*, Palm Beach Gardens, 1961
Perspective rendering of patio
Pencil on paper, 15" x 11 ⅜"
George A. Smathers Libraries, University of Florida

Woronzow Residence, Coconut Grove, 1959 (unbuilt)
Perspective rendering of patio
Microfilm
George A. Smathers Libraries, University of Florida

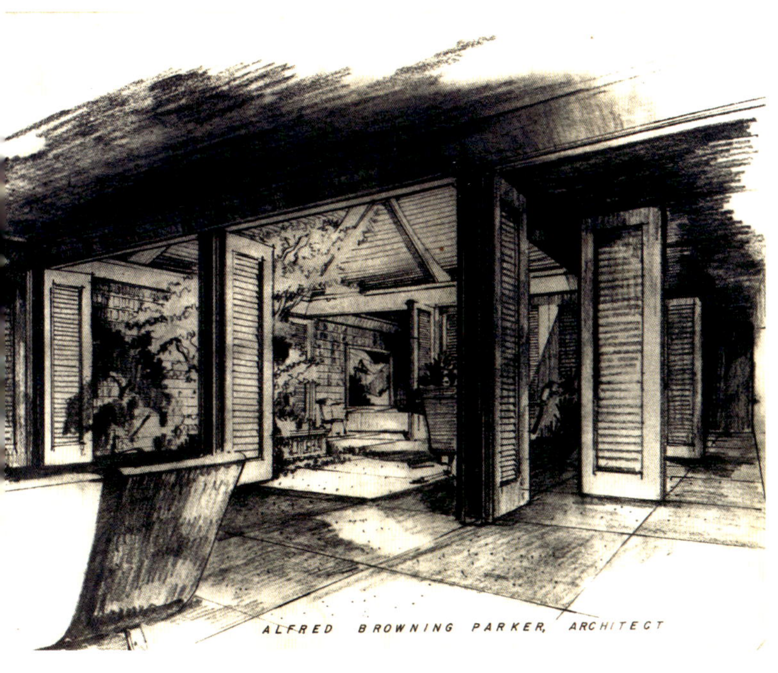
ALFRED BROWNING PARKER, ARCHITECT

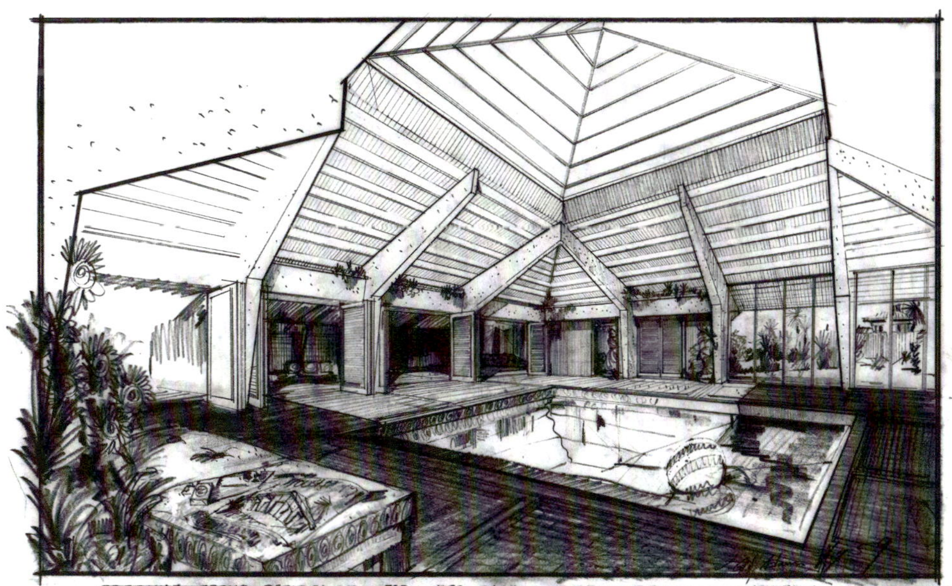
COCONUT GROVE RESIDENCE FOR MRS. BACHOO WORONZOW.
ARCHITECT ALFRED BROWNING PARKER

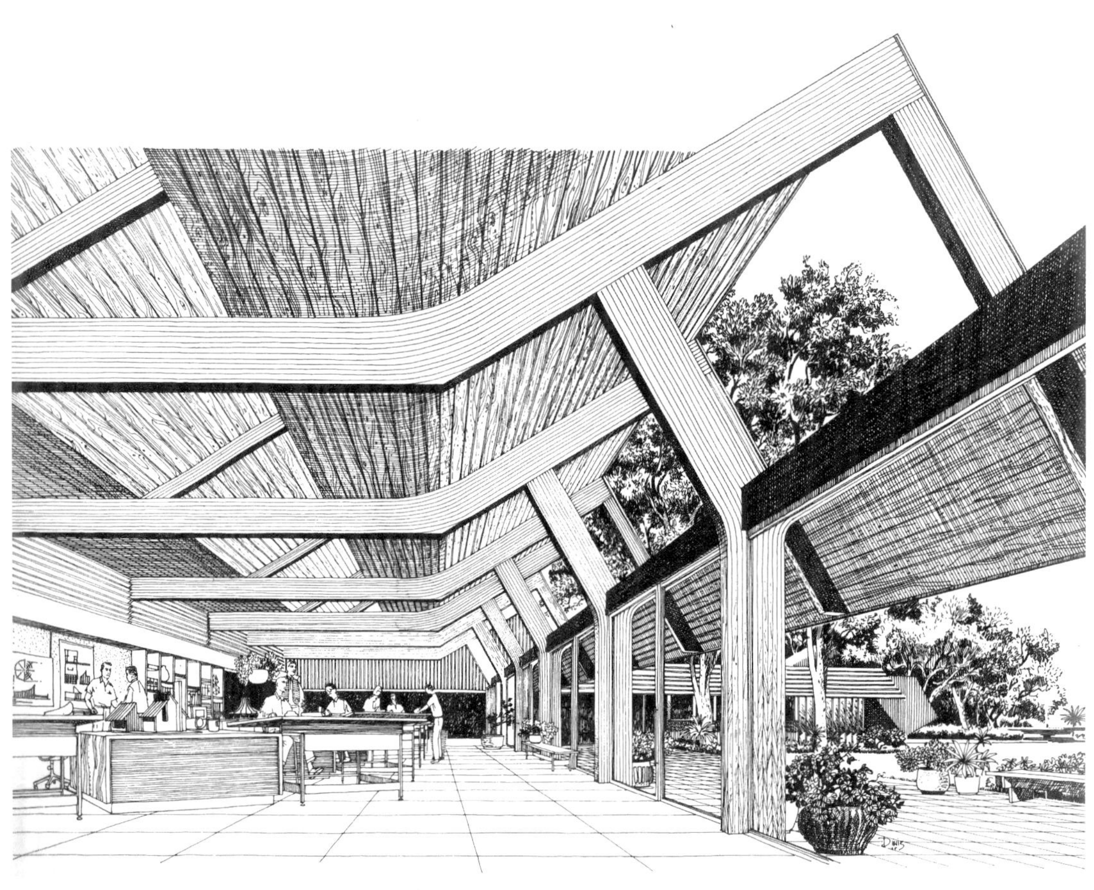

Concept for Architect's Office, commissioned by the Weyerhaeuser Company, Coconut Grove, 1965 (unbuilt)
Interior perspective rendering, signed Carlos Diniz, 24" x 24"
George A. Smathers Libraries, University of Florida

Alfred Browning Parker Office Workshop, Coconut Grove, 1967
Drafting room
B&W vintage photograph, 8" x 10"
Arva Moore Parks

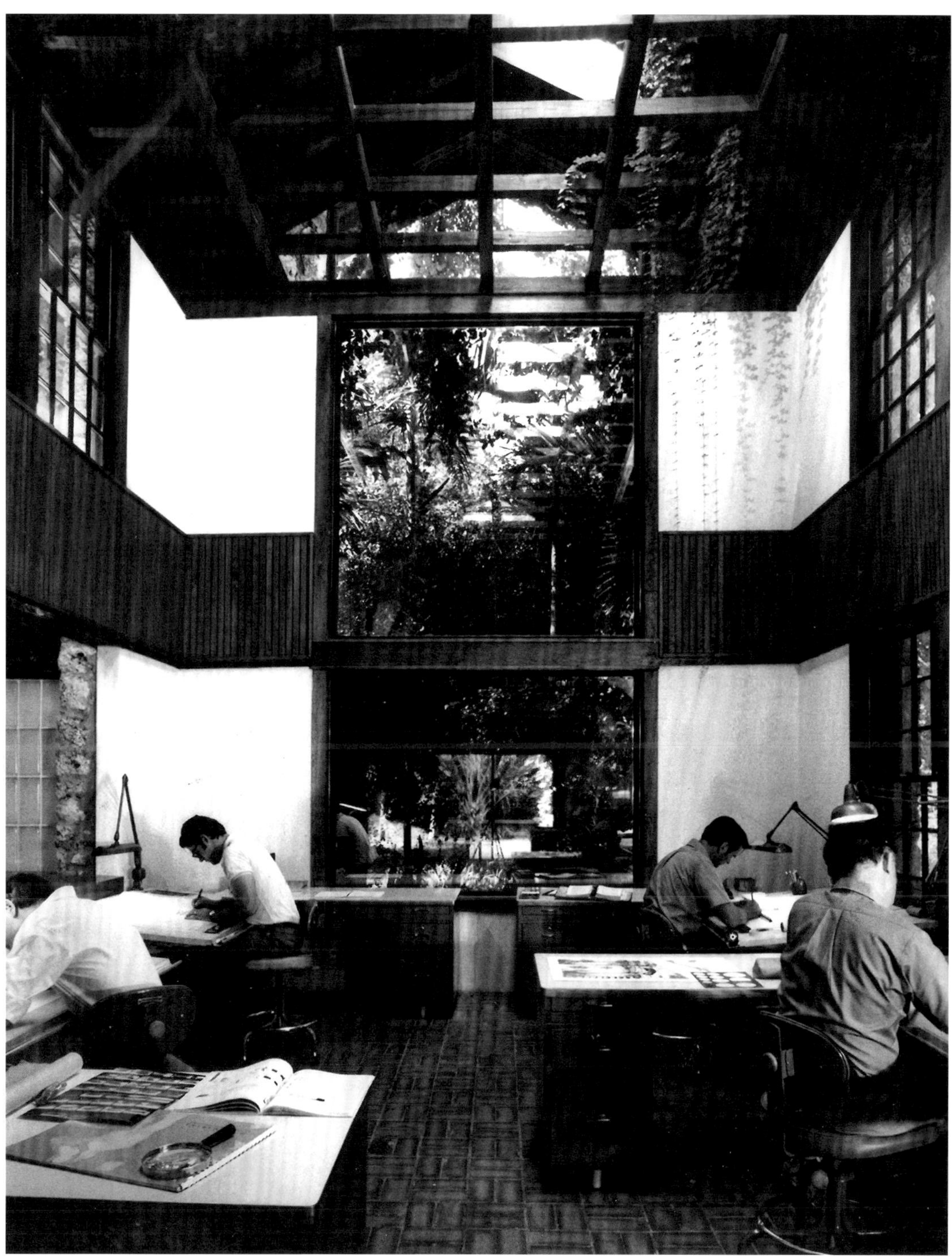

Part IV
Monumentality and Social Engagement (1962-1972)

Groves Residence, Freeport, Grand Bahama Island, 1959
Photograph © Ezra Stoller/ESTO
ESTO

***House Beautiful*, January 1964**
Magazine, 9 ½" x 12 ½"
Cover photograph of Groves Residence, 1959
Photograph © Ezra Stoller/ESTO
Courtesy of Randolph C. Henning

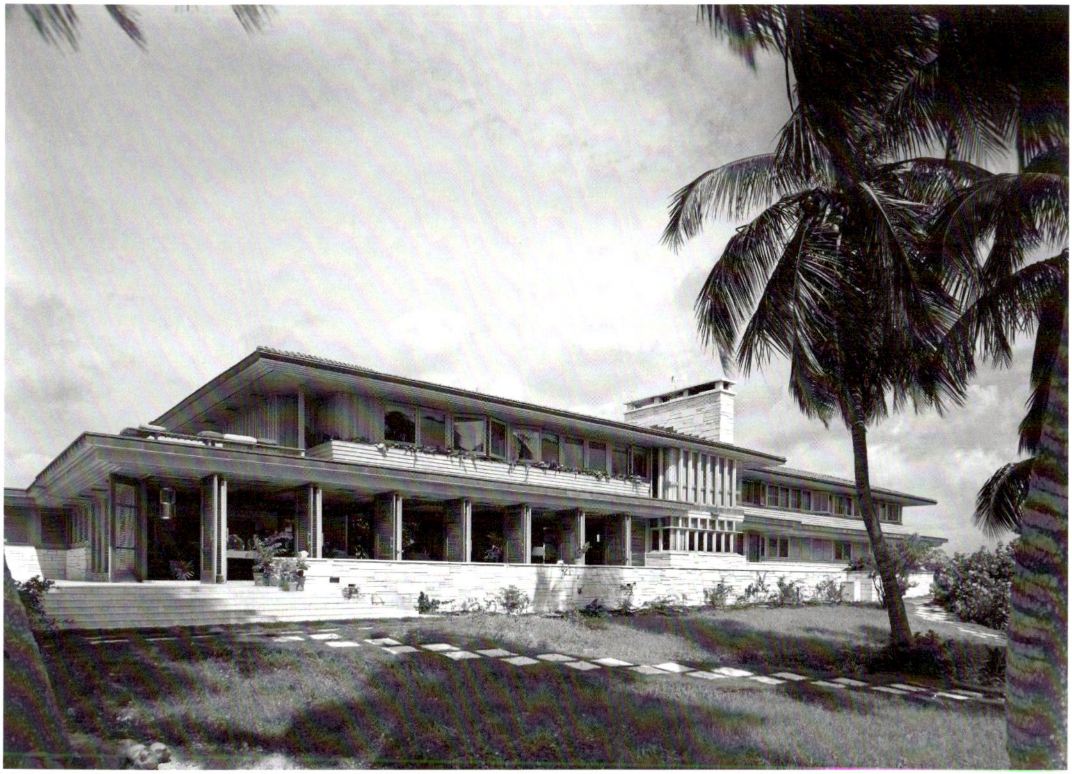

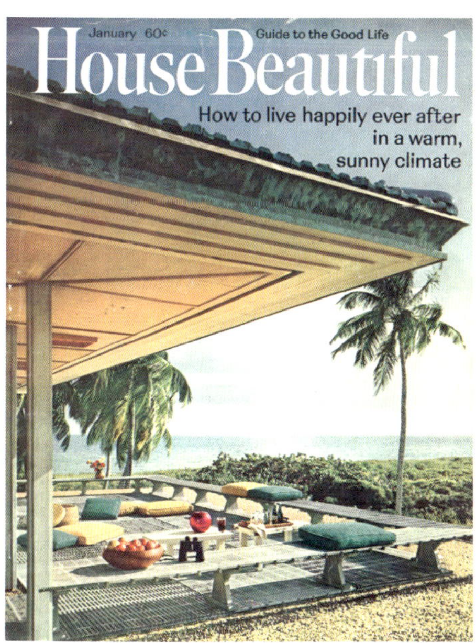
January 60¢
Guide to the Good Life
House Beautiful
How to live happily ever after
in a warm,
sunny climate

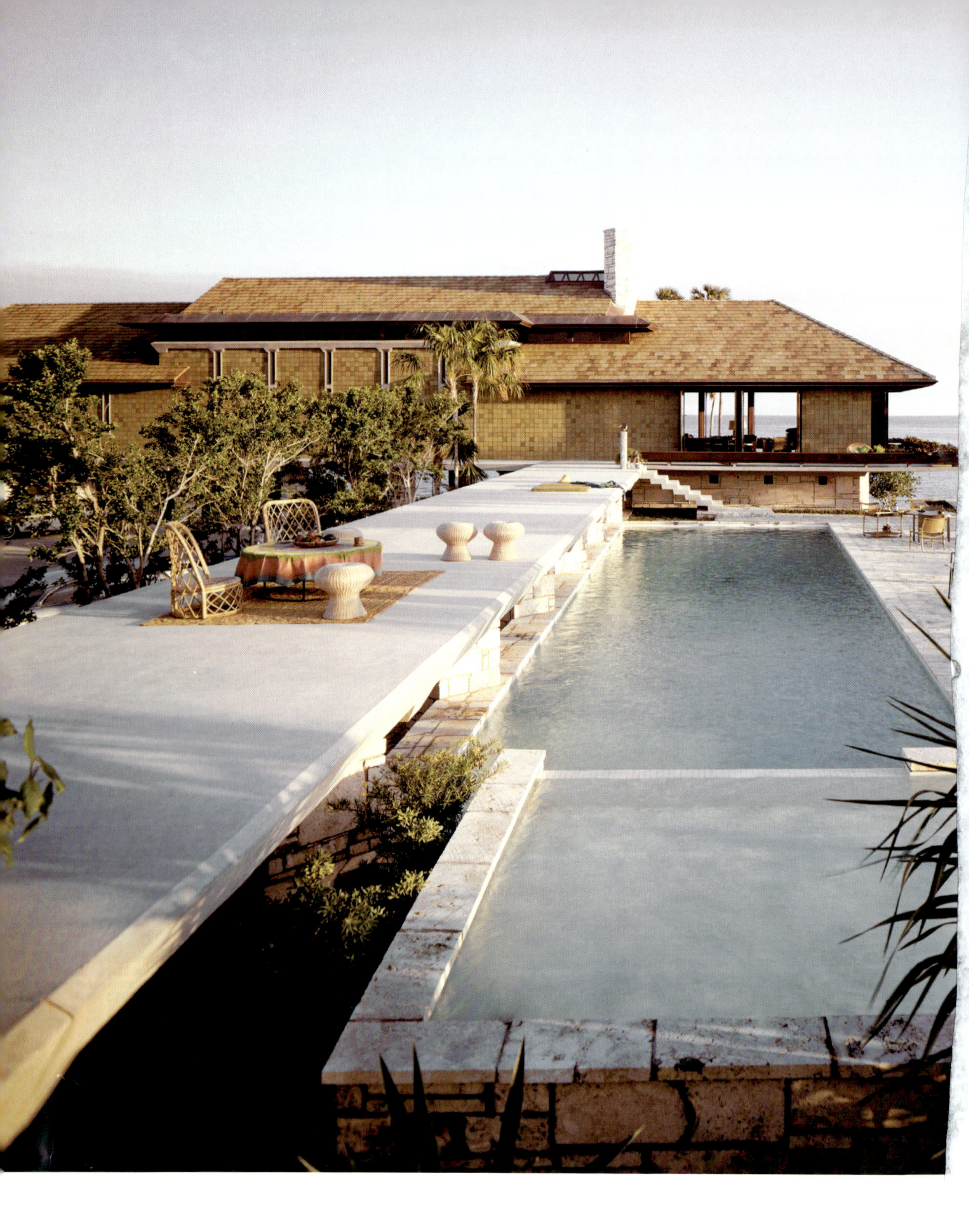

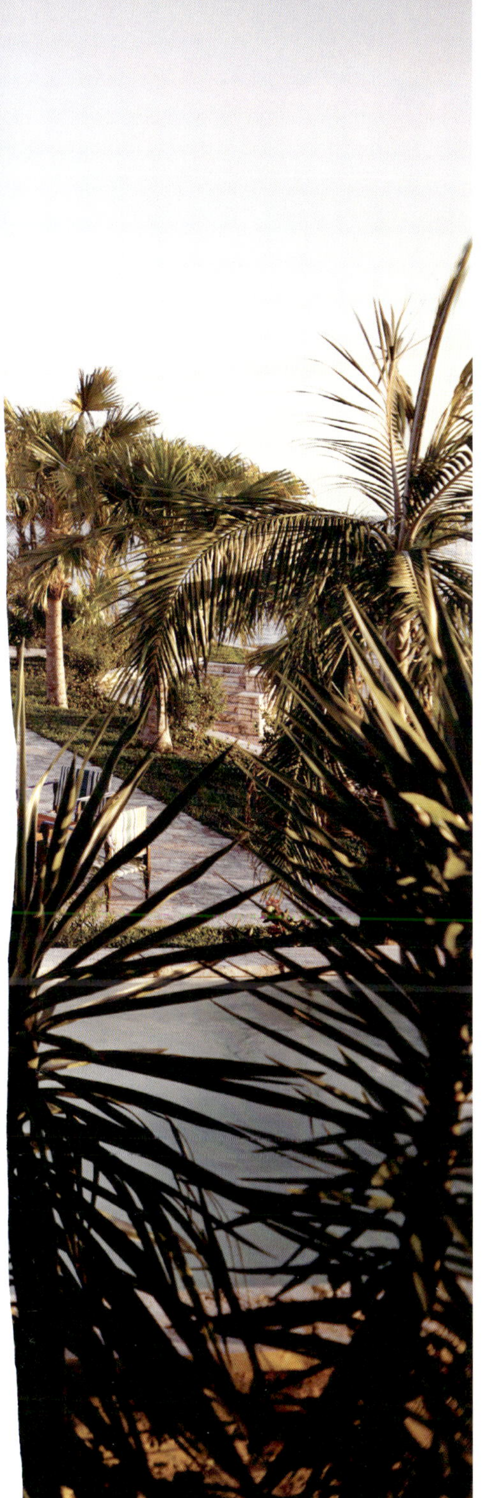

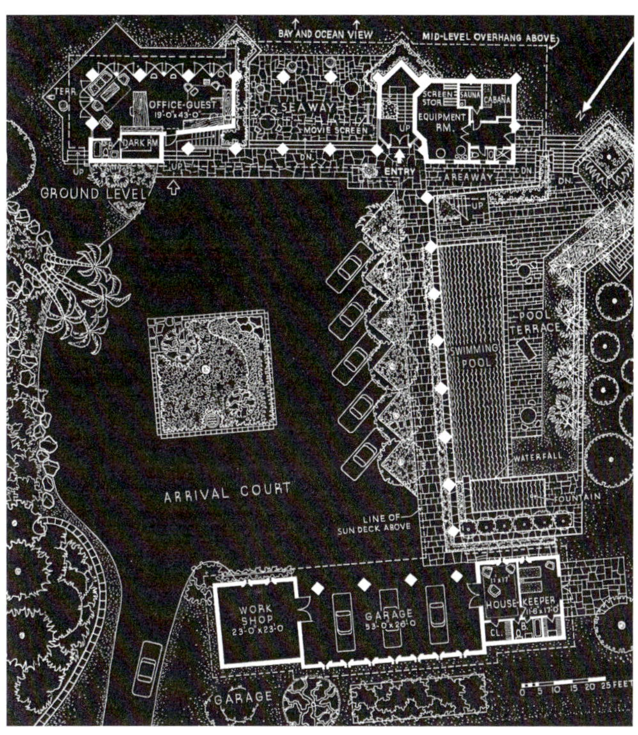

Parker Residence (1965 Pace Setter), Gables Estates, Coral Gables, 1962
Pool terrace
Photograph © Ezra Stoller/ESTO
ESTO

Parker Residence (1965 Pace Setter), Gables Estates, Coral Gables, 1962
Excerpt from *House Beautiful*, May 1965
Site plan, 9 ½" x 12 ½"
Courtesy of Randolph C. Henning

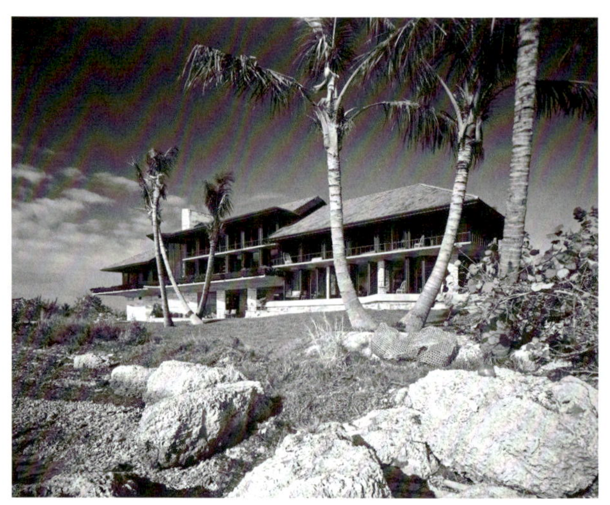

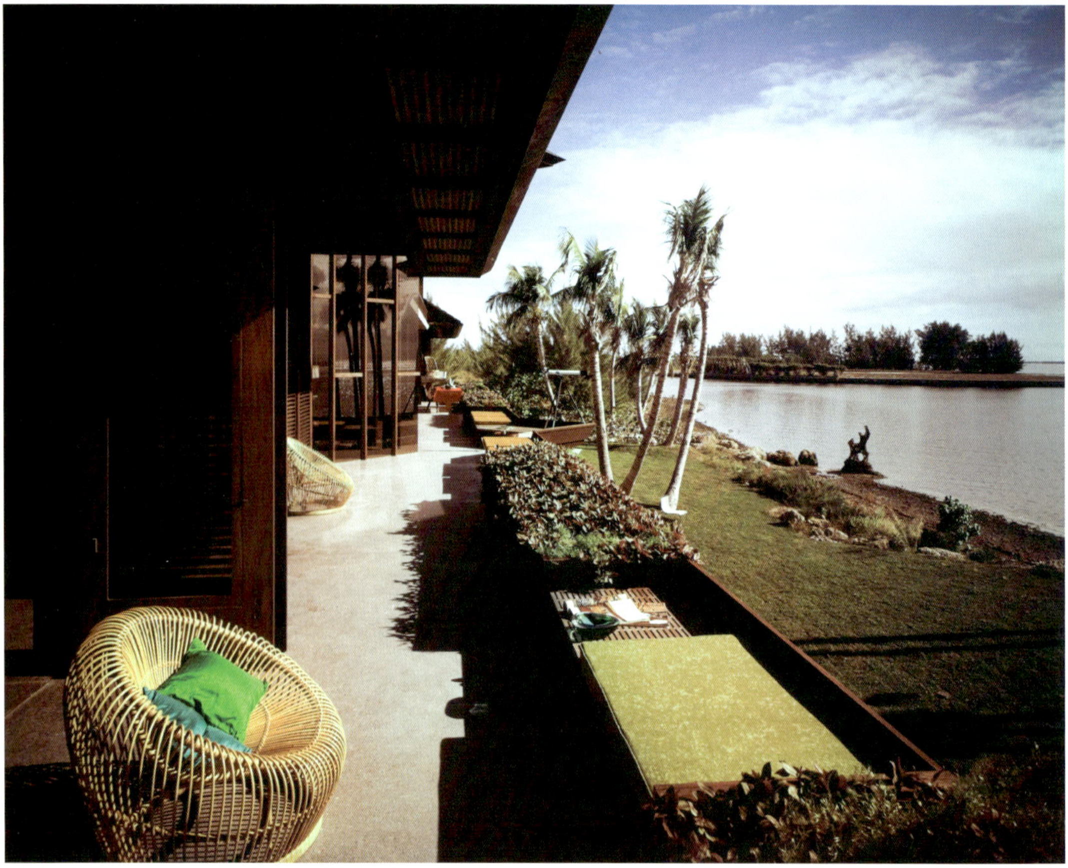

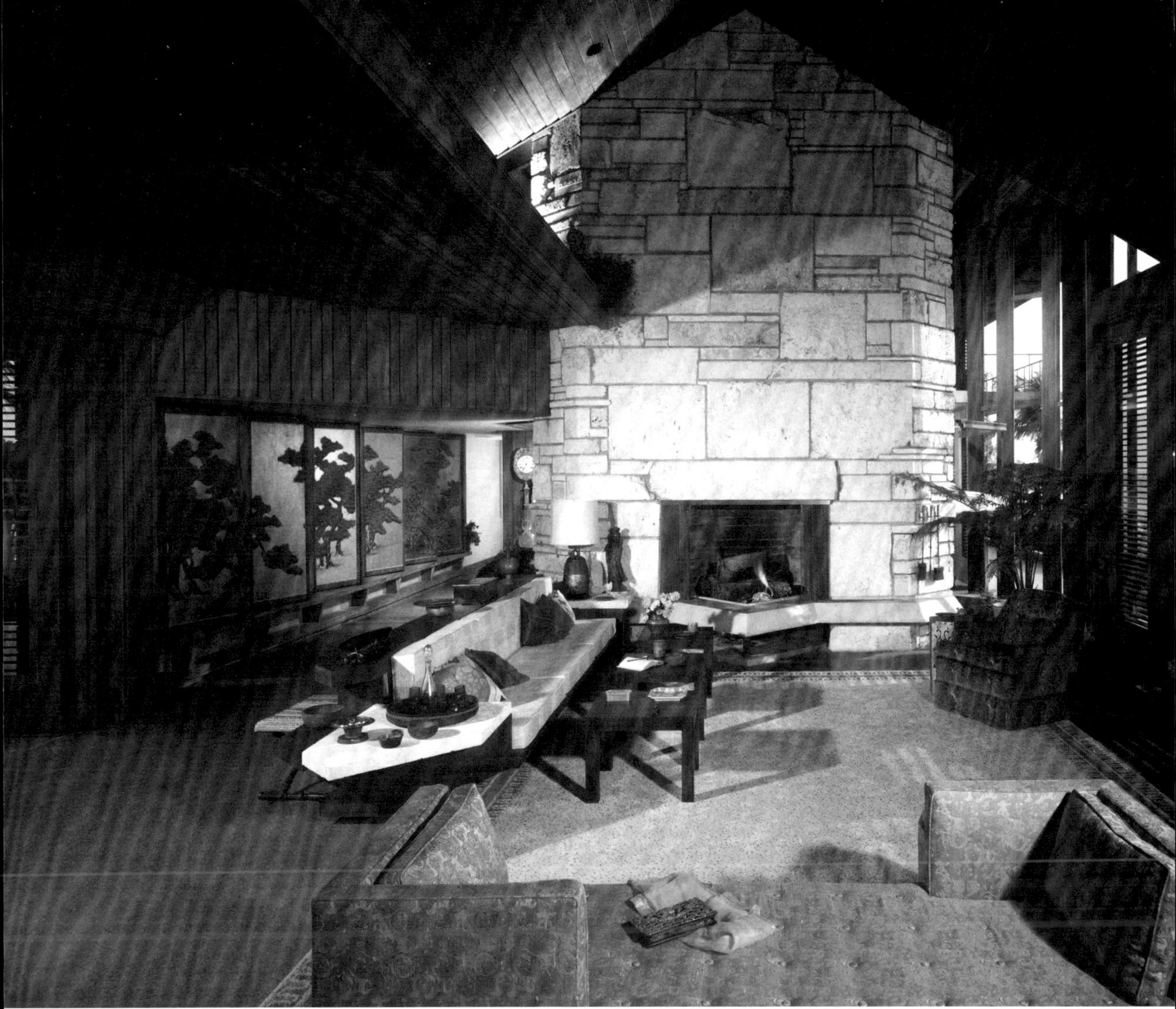

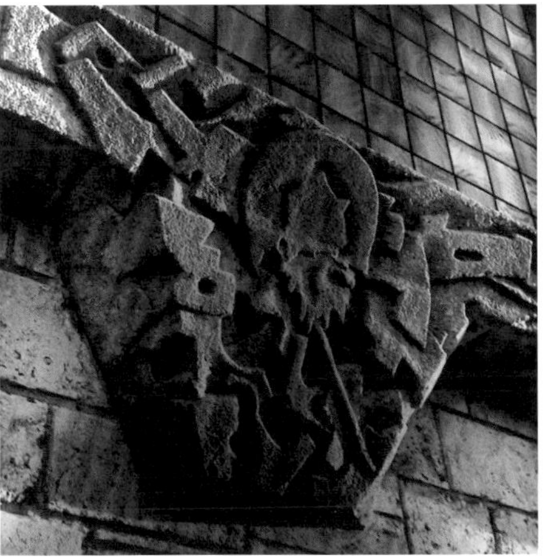

Parker Residence (Pace Setter 1965), Gables Estates, Coral Gables, 1962
Photograph © Ezra Stoller/ESTO
ESTO

Parker Residence (Pace Setter 1965), Gables Estates, Coral Gables, 1962
Waterfront terrace
Photograph © Ezra Stoller/ESTO
ESTO

Parker Residence (Pace Setter 1965), Gables Estates, Coral Gables, 1962
Living area
B&W vintage photograph, 9 ½" x 7 ⅝"
Photograph © Ezra Stoller/ESTO
Courtesy of Randolph C. Henning

Parker Residence (Pace Setter 1965), Gables Estates, Coral Gables, 1962
Corbels sculpture by Albert Vrana
B&W vintage photograph, 8 ½" x 11"
Photograph © Ezra Stoller/ESTO
George A. Smathers Libraries, University of Florida

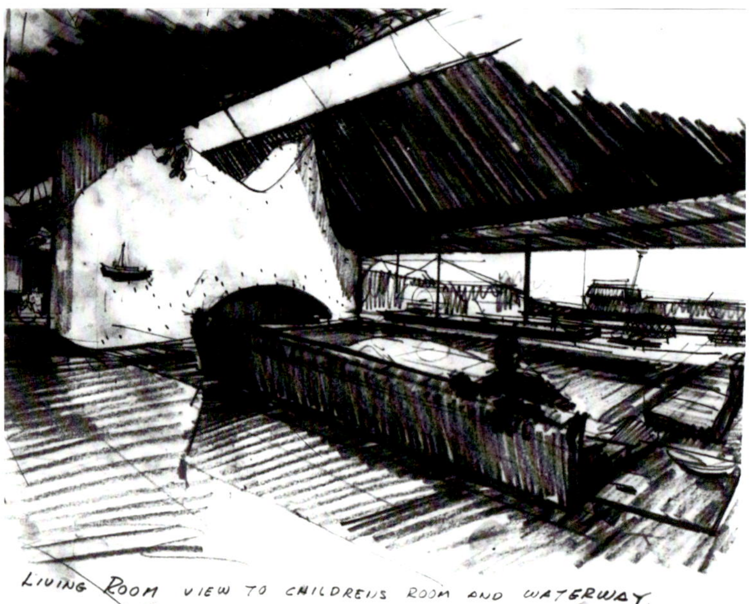

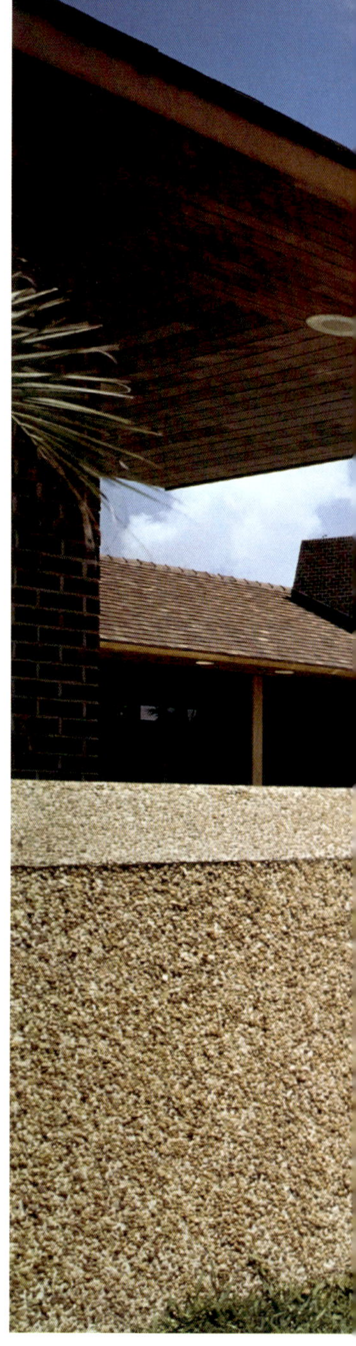

Landon Residence, Gables Estates, Coral Gables, 1965
Living area, view to children's room and waterway
Microfilm
George A. Smathers Libraries, University of Florida

Landon Residence, Gables Estates, Coral Gables, 1965
Photograph © Ezra Stoller/ESTO
ESTO

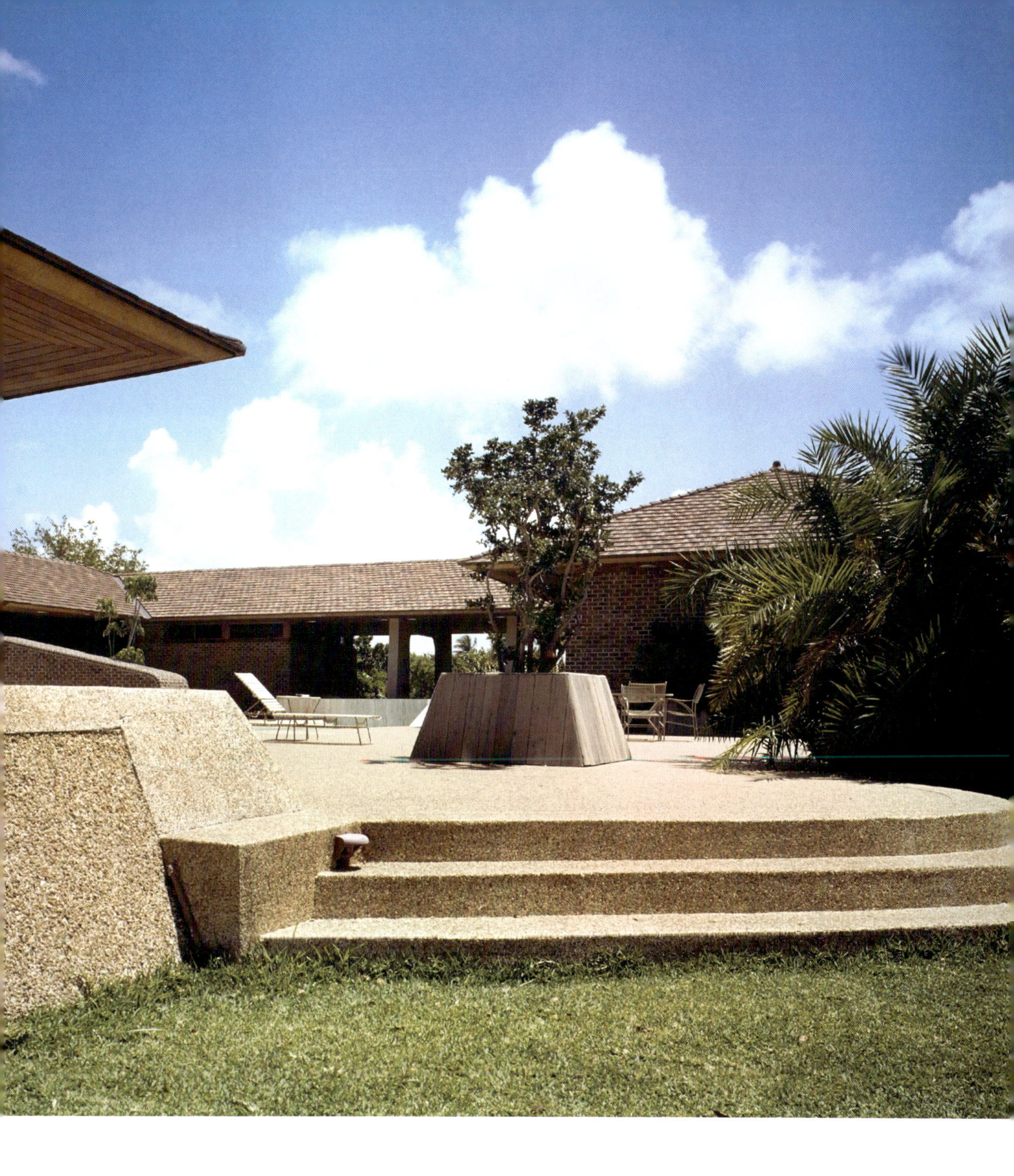

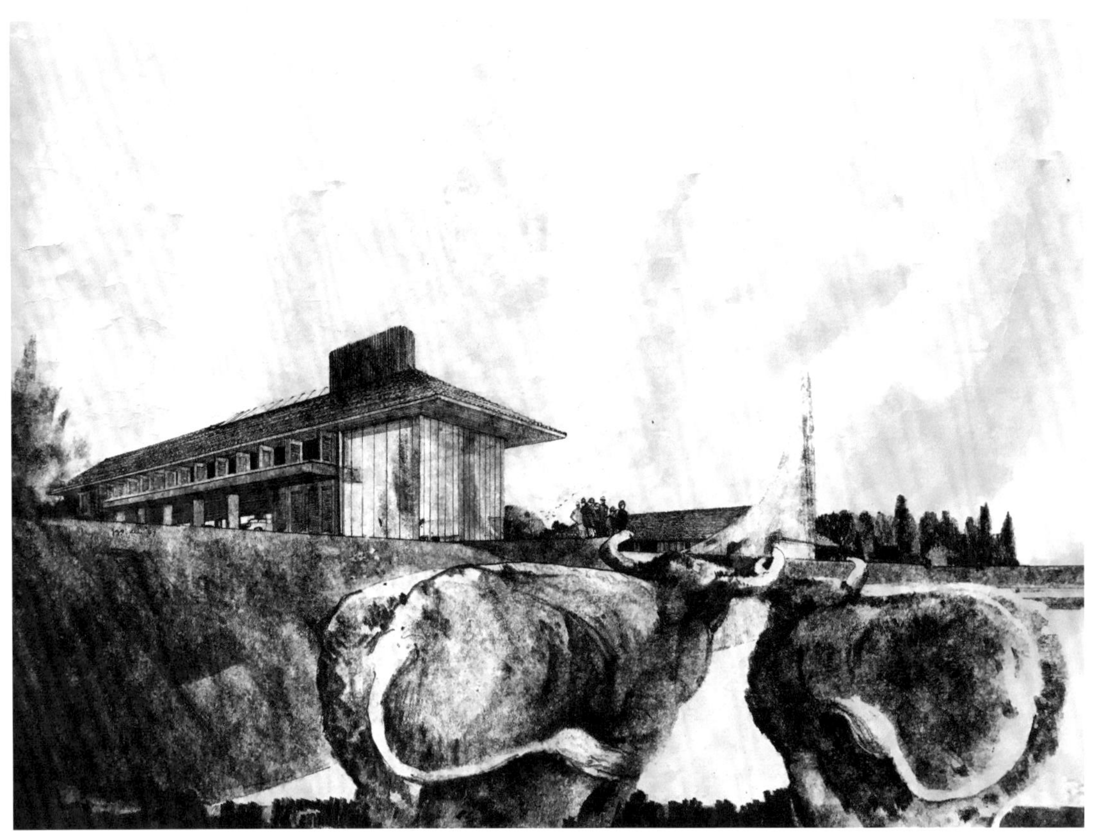

Big B Ranch (Beinecke Residence), Belle Glade, 1970 (partially built)
Manager's residence
Perspective rendering
Printed ephemera, 20" x 15 ⅞"
Courtesy of Henry Alexander

House of God, Vista Memorial Gardens, Miami Lakes, 1958
Perspective
Microfilm
George A. Smathers Libraries, University of Florida

House of God, Vista Memorial Gardens, Miami Lakes, 1958
Vintage color photograph, 10" x 8"
Photograph © Kurt Weldmann
George A. Smathers Libraries, University of Florida

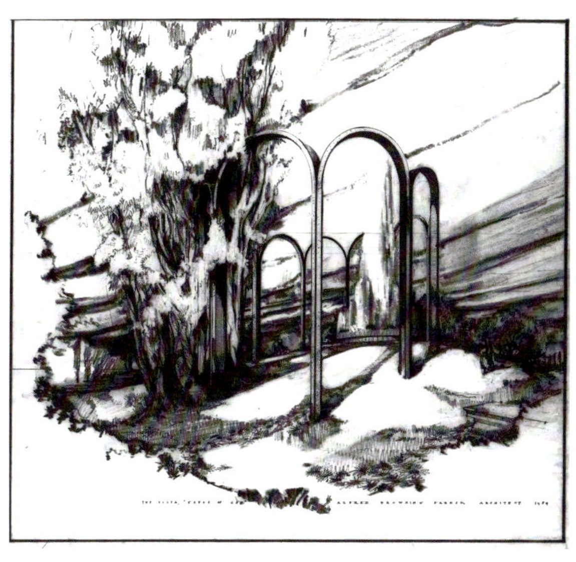

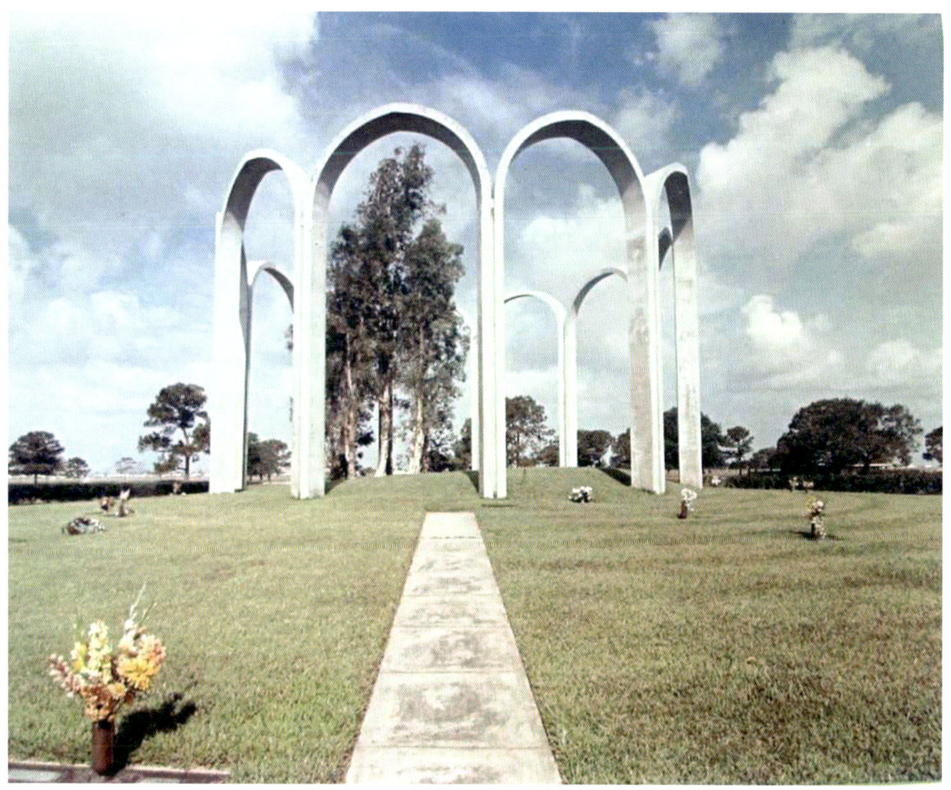

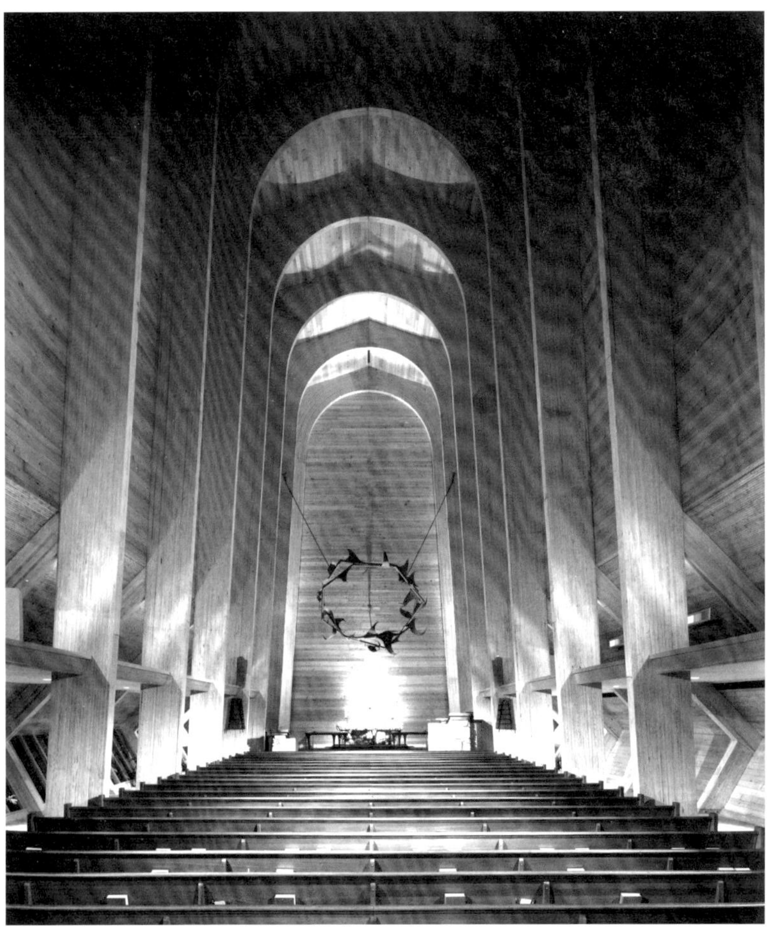

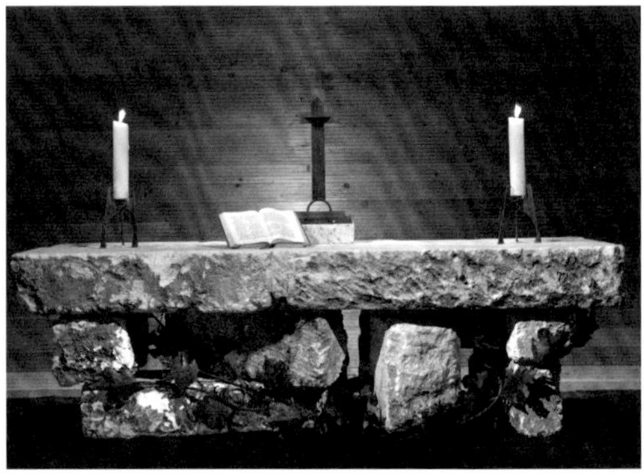

Hope Lutheran Church Sanctuary, South Miami, 1962
Church nave with "Crown of Thorns" by sculptor Albert Vrana
B&W vintage photograph, 13 ½" x 14"
Photograph © Ezra Stoller/ESTO
Courtesy of Randolph C. Henning

Hope Lutheran Church Sanctuary, South Miami, 1962
Stone altar
B&W vintage photograph, 12 ⅛" x 14"
Photograph © Ezra Stoller/ESTO
Courtesy of Randolph C. Henning

Hope Lutheran Church Sanctuary, South Miami, 1962
Photograph © Ezra Stoller/ESTO
ESTO

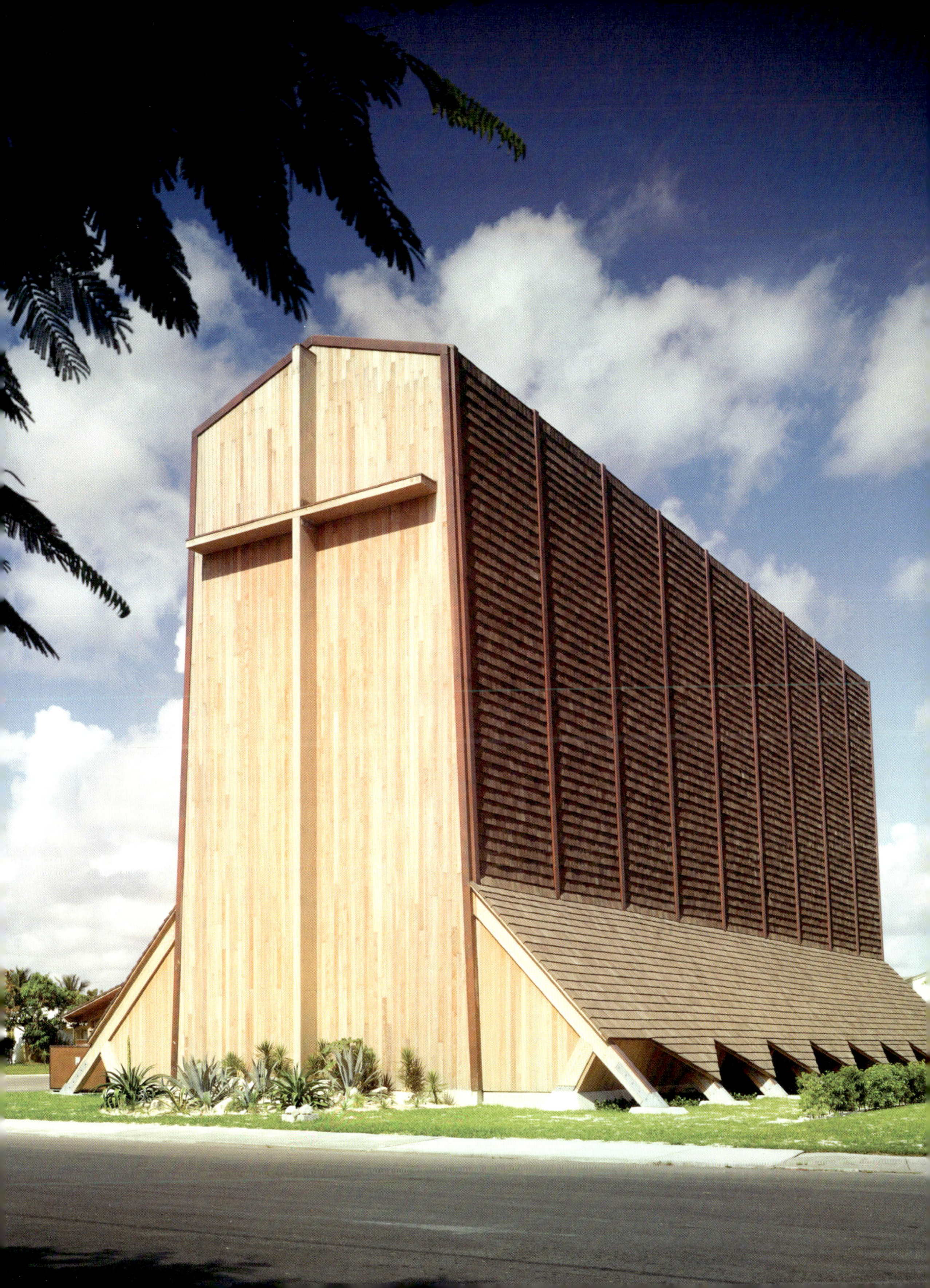

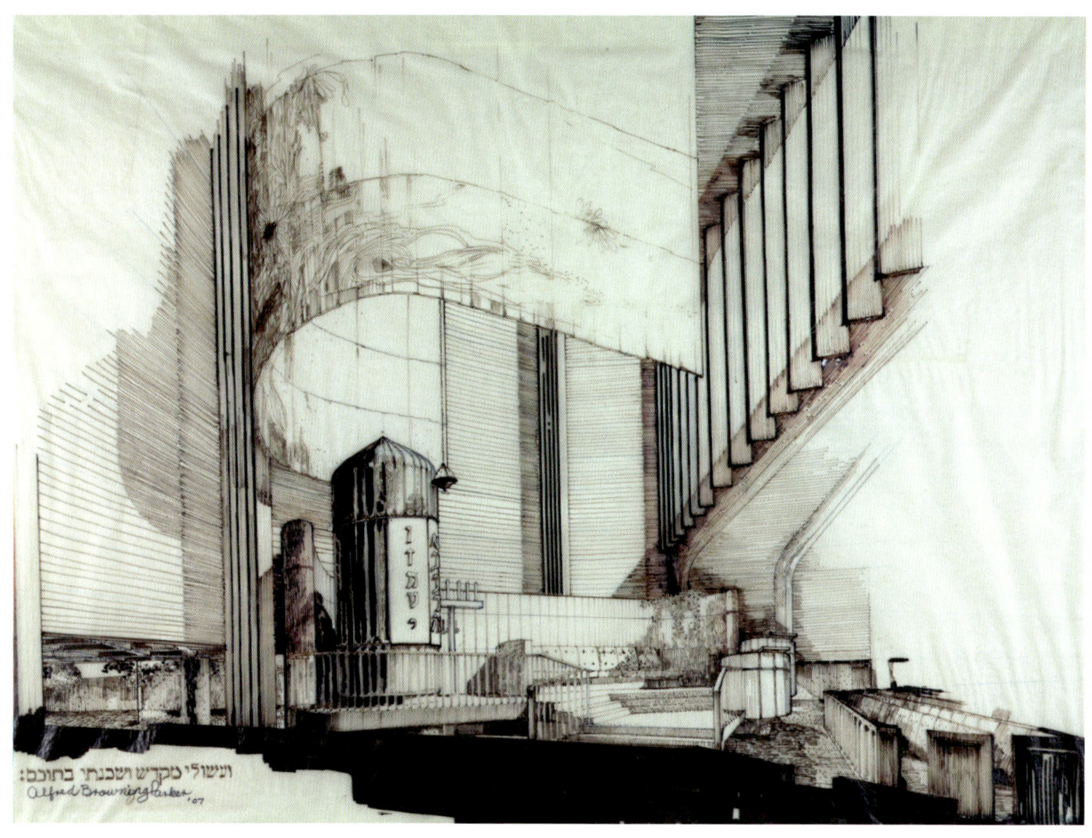

Fread Sanctuary at Temple Beth El, West Palm Beach, 1971
Interior perspective rendering of Bima
Ink on trace paper, 36" x 28"
George A. Smathers Libraries, University of Florida

Fread Sanctuary at Temple Beth El, West Palm Beach, 1971
Photograph © Bo Parker
Courtesy of Randolph C. Henning

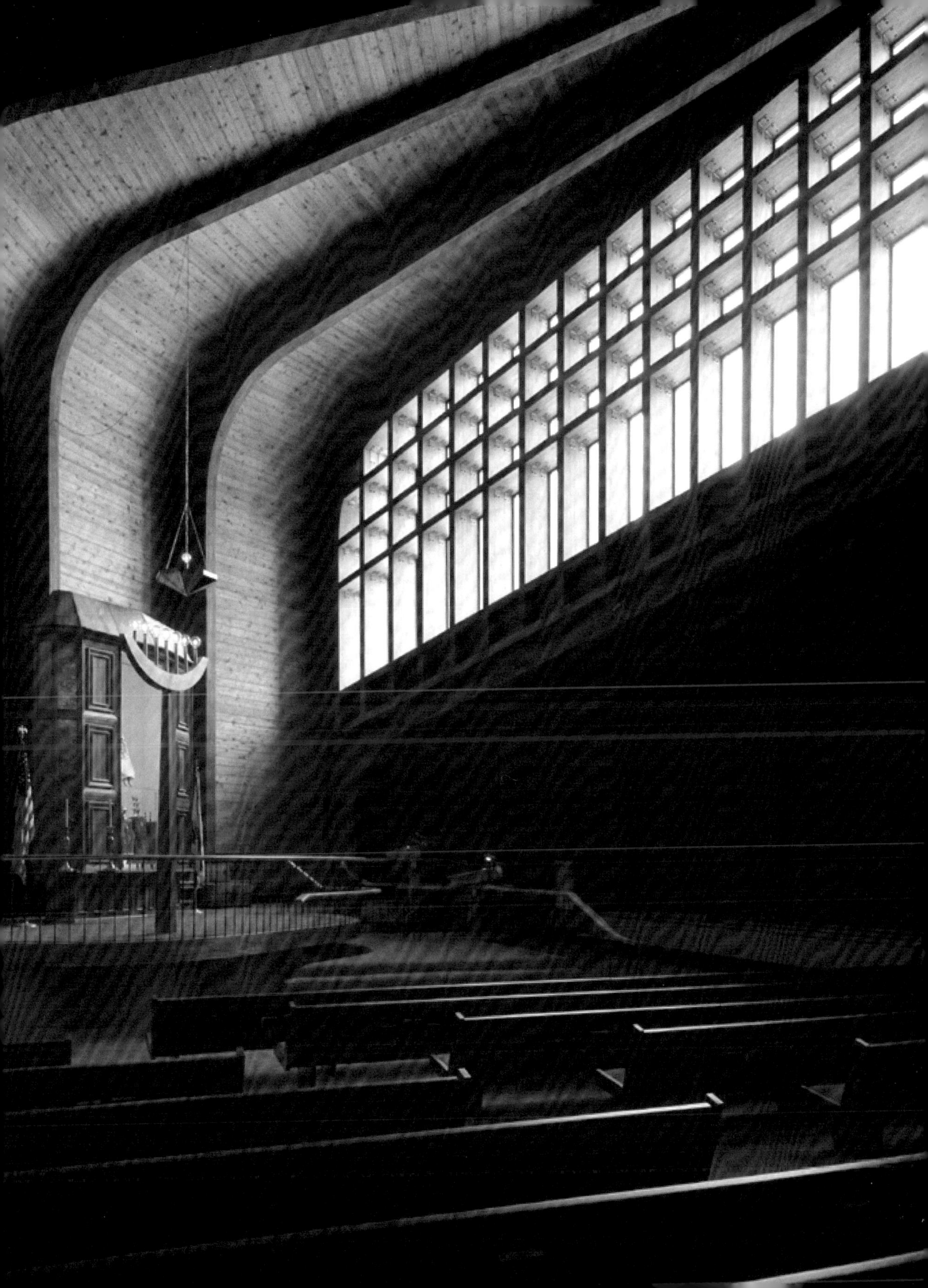

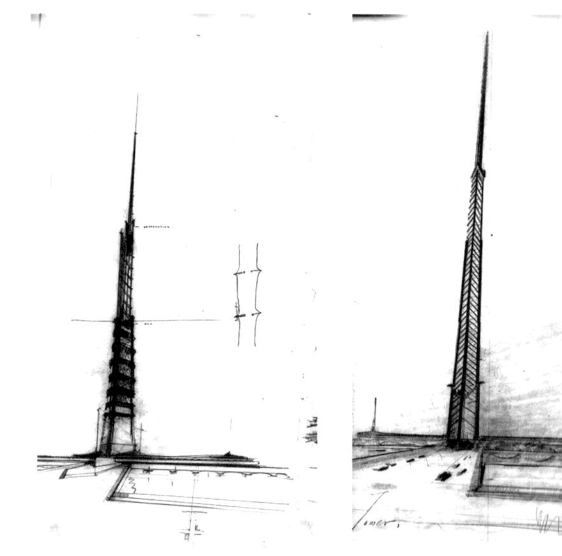

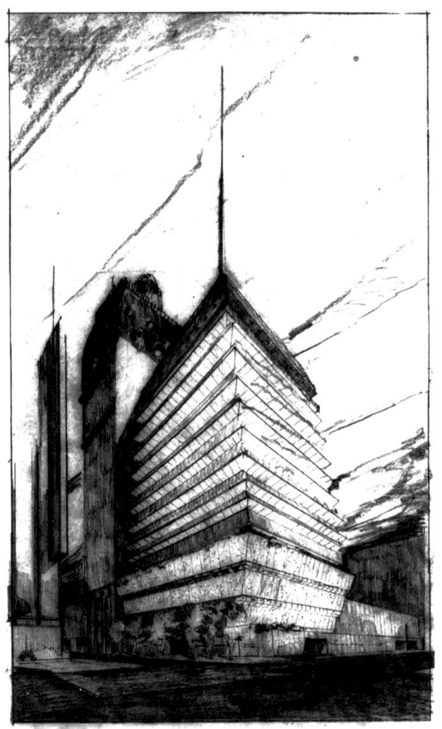

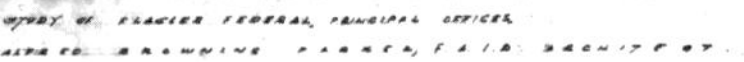
STUDY OF FLAGLER FEDERAL PRINCIPAL OFFICES
ALFRED BROWNING PARKER, F.A.I.A. ARCHITECT

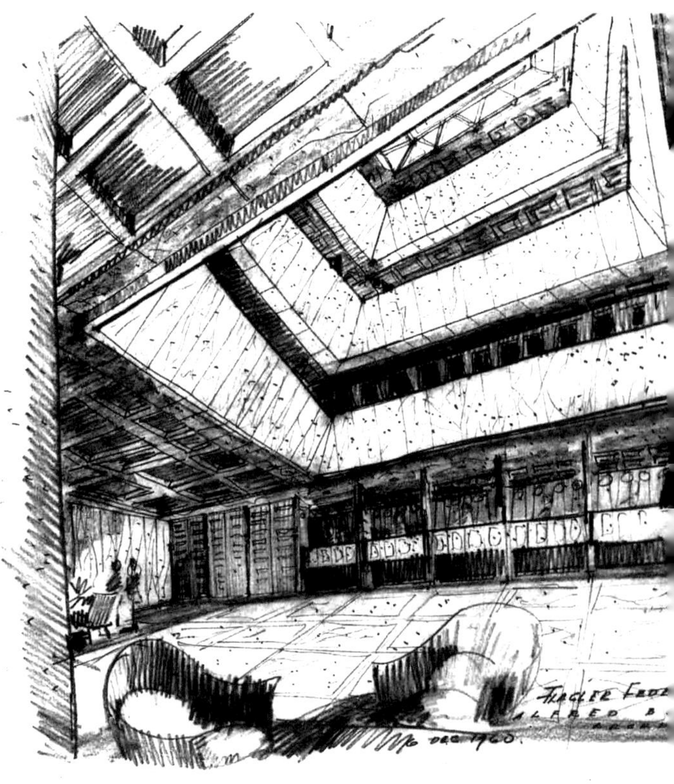
10 DEC 1960

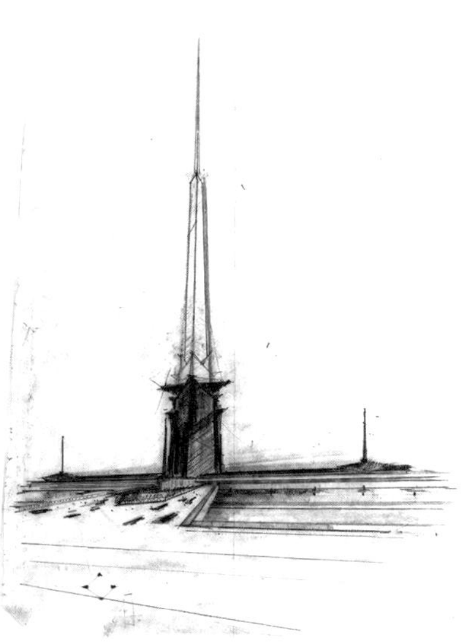

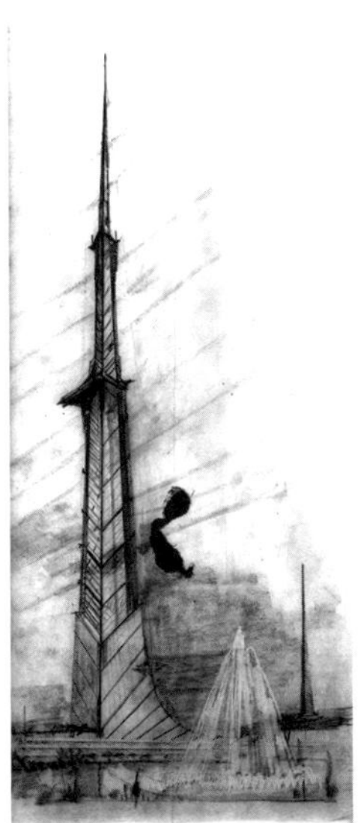

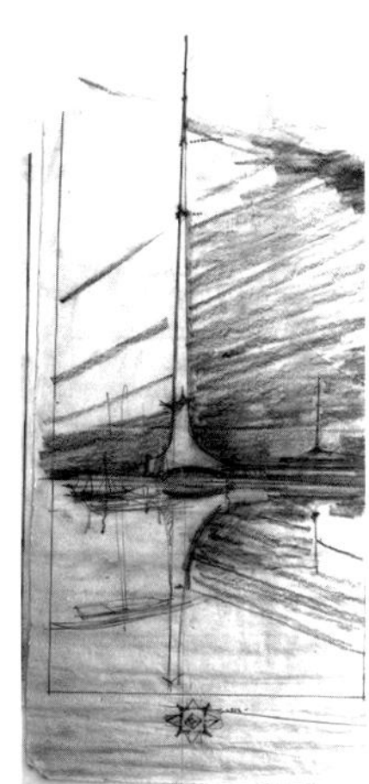

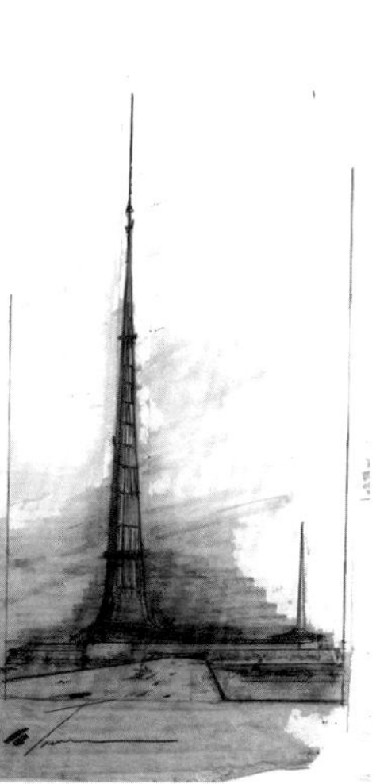

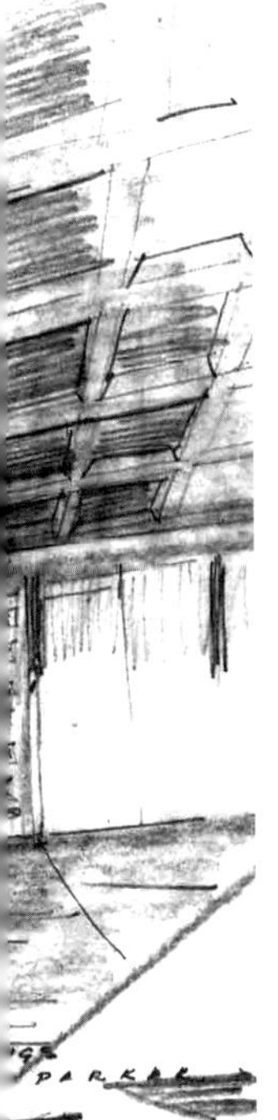

Fort Lauderdale Tower, Fort Lauderdale, 1965 (unbuilt)
Studies
Microfilm
George A. Smathers Libraries, University of Florida

Flagler Federal Savings & Loan – Main Office, Miami, 1961
Perspective rendering
Microfilm
George A. Smathers Libraries, University of Florida

Flagler Federal Savings & Loan – Main Office, Miami, 1961
Perspective rendering of bank lobby
Microfilm
George A. Smathers Libraries, University of Florida

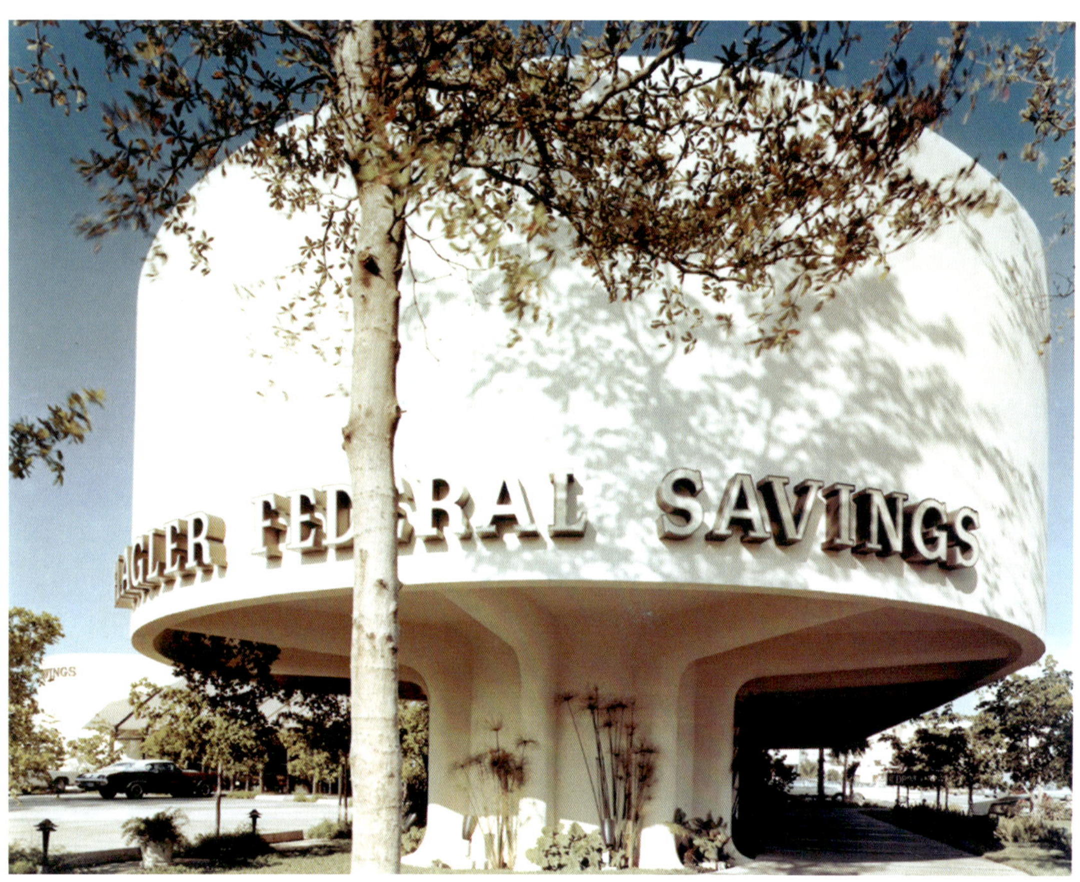

Flagler Federal Savings & Loan, North Miami Beach Branch, 1969
Color vintage photograph, 8" x 10"
Courtesy of Randolph C. Henning

Fort Lauderdale Theater, Galt Ocean Mile, Fort Lauderdale, 1959 (unbuilt)
Perspective rendering, 16" x 9"
Excerpt from *Fort Lauderdale Playhouse* brochure, 1960-61 season
George A. Smathers Libraries, University of Florida

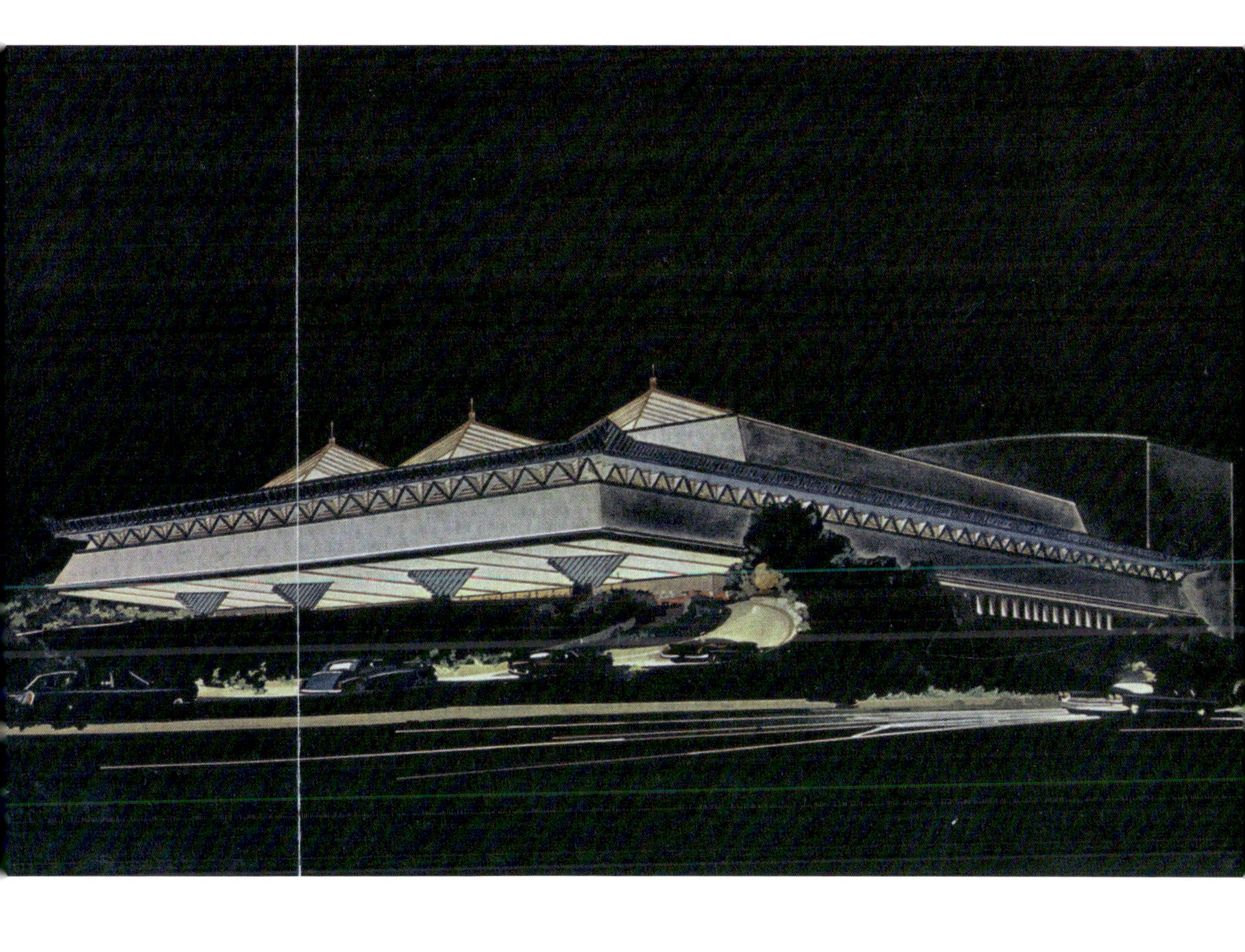

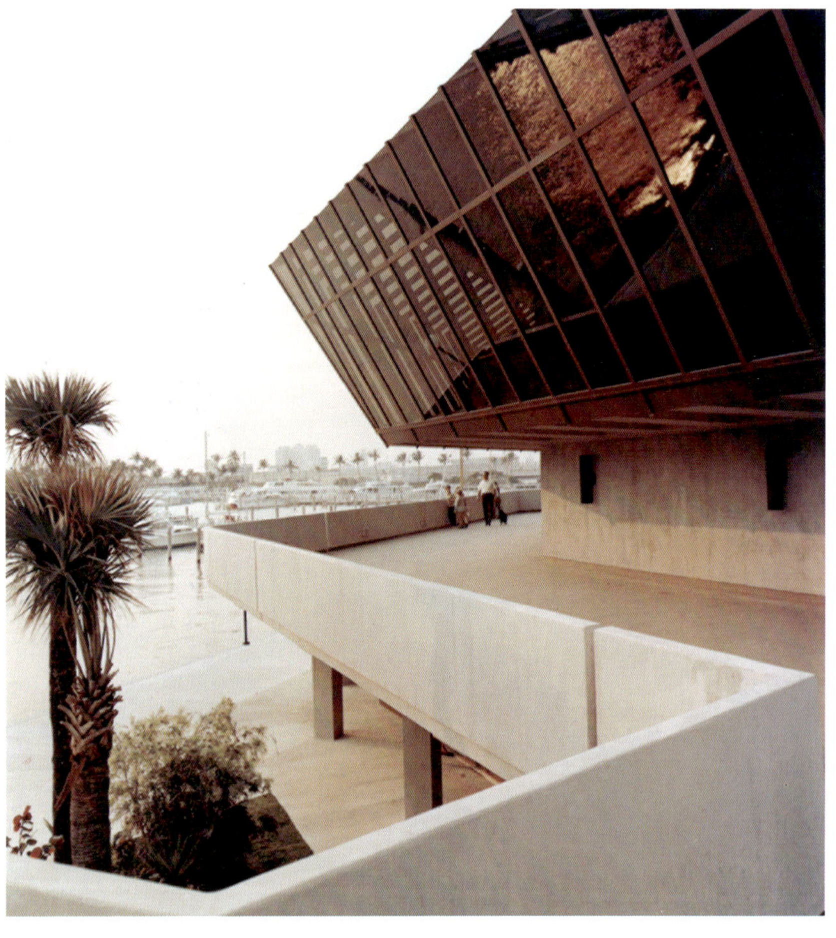

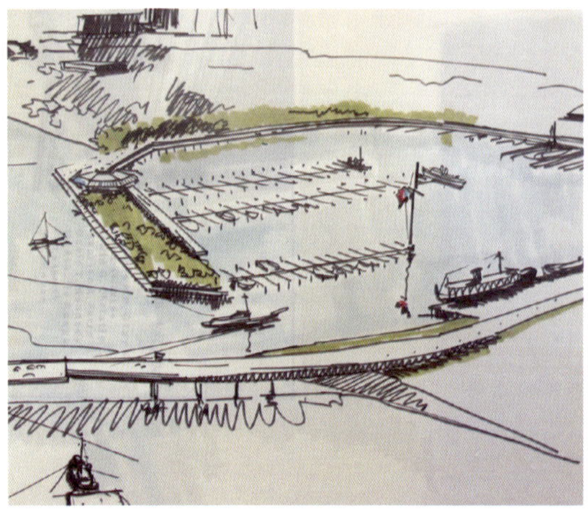

Miamarina, Miami, 1966
Upper level concourse
Color vintage photograph, 7 ¾" x 9 ⅛"
Photograph © Ezra Stoller/ESTO
Courtesy of Randolph C. Henning

Miamarina, Miami, 1966
Aerial perspective view
Ink and magic marker on trace paper, 17" x 14"
George A. Smathers Libraries, University of Florida

Miamarina, Miami, 1966
Dining area
Color vintage photograph, 9 ¾" x 7 ¾"
Photograph © Ezra Stoller/ESTO
Courtesy of Randolph C. Henning

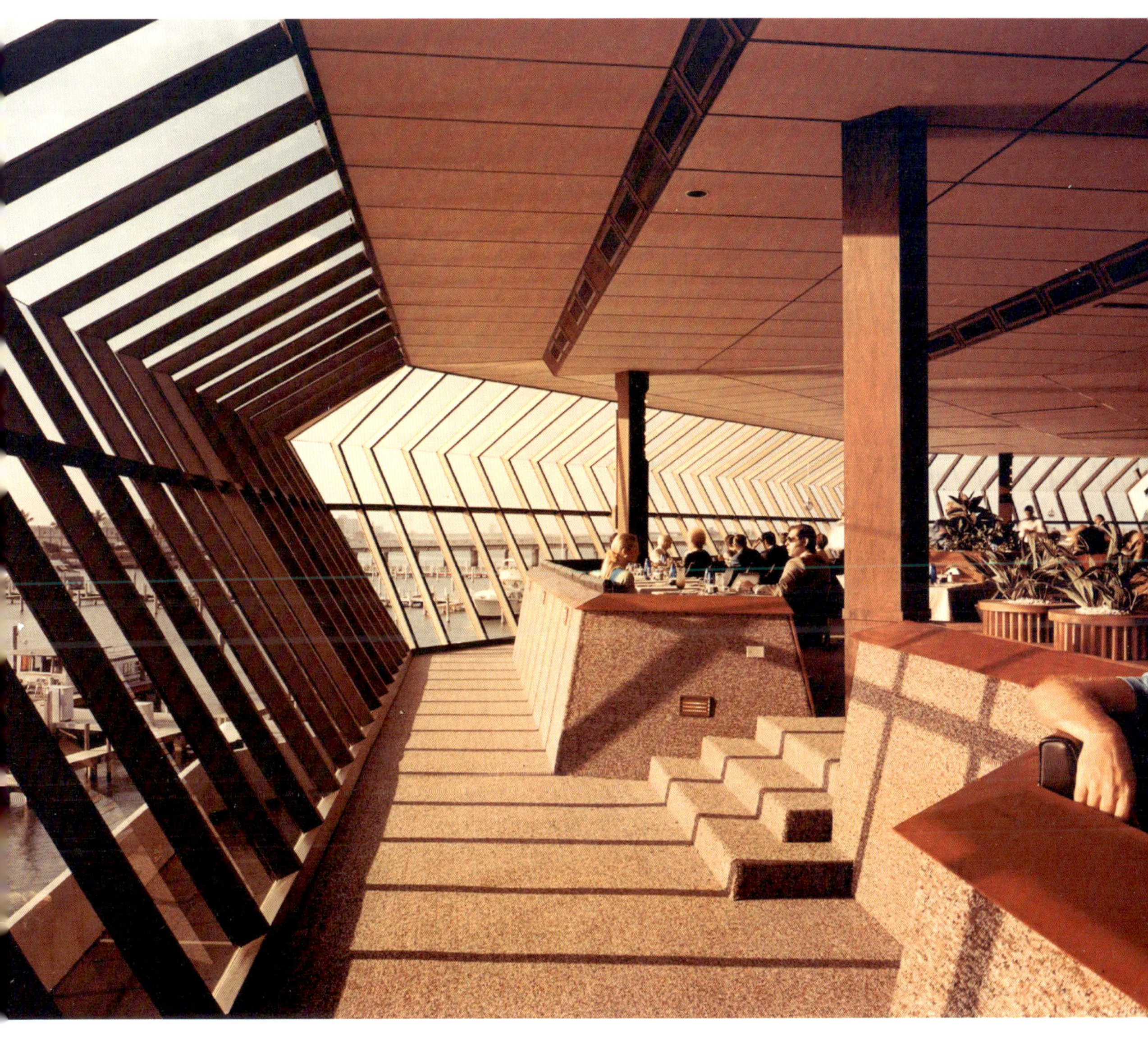

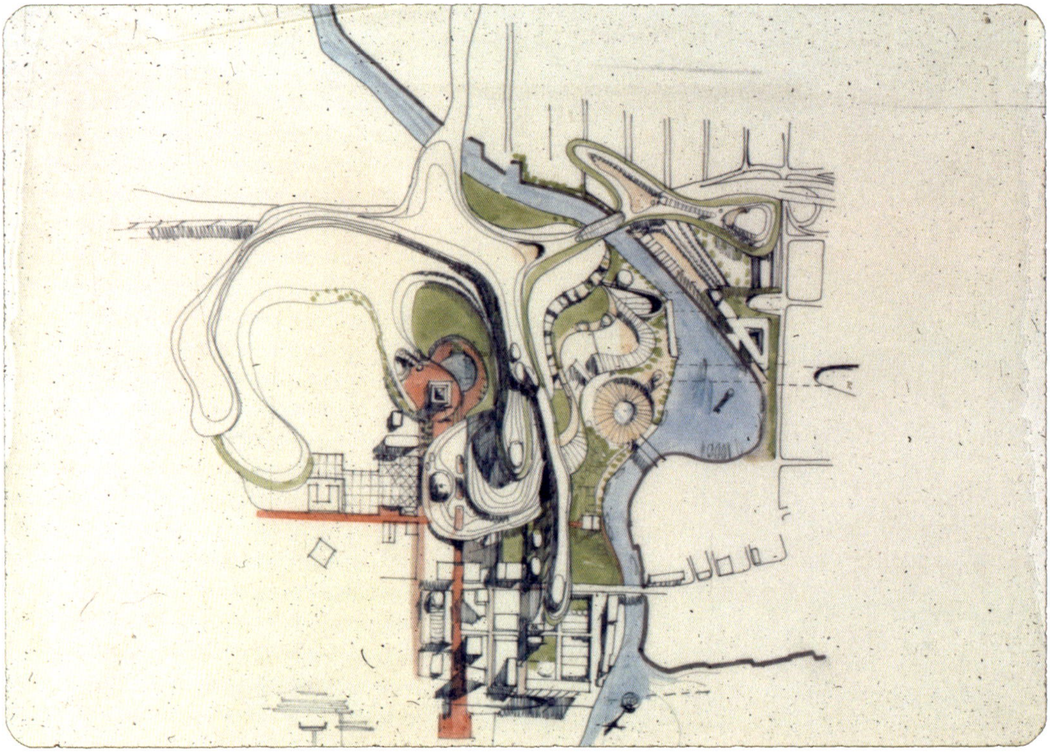

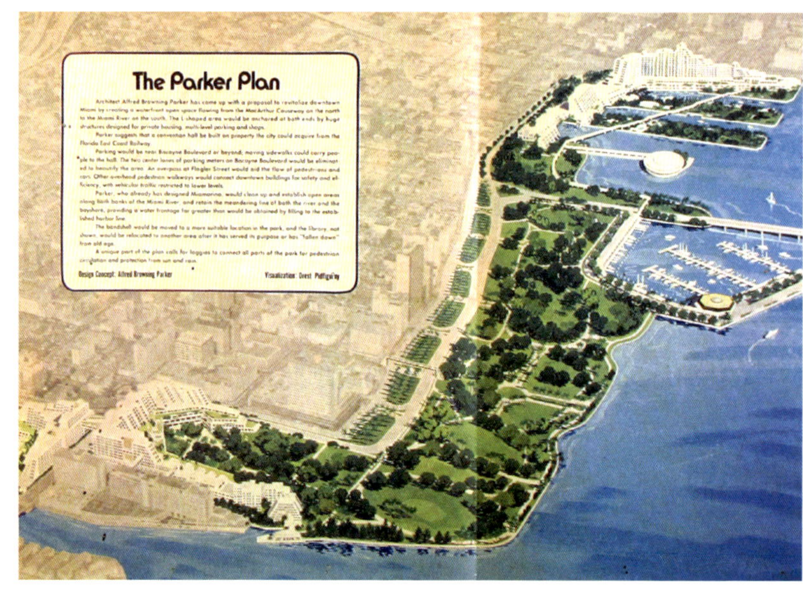
The Parker Plan
Architect Alfred Browning Parker has come up with a proposal to revitalize downtown Miami by creating a waterfront open space flowing from the MacArthur Causeway on the north to the Miami River on the south. The L-shaped area would be anchored at both ends by huge structures designed for private housing, multi-level parking and shops.
Parker suggests that a convention hall be built on property the city could acquire from the Florida East Coast Railway.
Parking would be near Biscayne Boulevard or beyond; moving sidewalks could carry people to the hall. The two center lanes of parking meters on Biscayne Boulevard would be eliminated to beautify the area. An overpass at Flagler Street would aid the flow of pedestrians and cars. Other overhead pedestrian walkways would connect downtown buildings for safety and efficiency, with vehicular traffic restricted to lower levels.
Parker, who already has designed Miamarina, would clean up and establish open areas along both banks of the Miami River, and retain the meandering line of both the river and the bayshore, providing a water frontage far greater than would be obtained by filling to the established harbor line.
The bandshell would be moved to a more suitable location in the park, and the library, not shown, would be relocated to another area after it has served its purpose or has "fallen down" from old age.
A unique part of the plan calls for loggias to connect all parts of the park for pedestrian circulation and protection from sun and rain.
Design Concept: Alfred Browning Parker
Visualization:

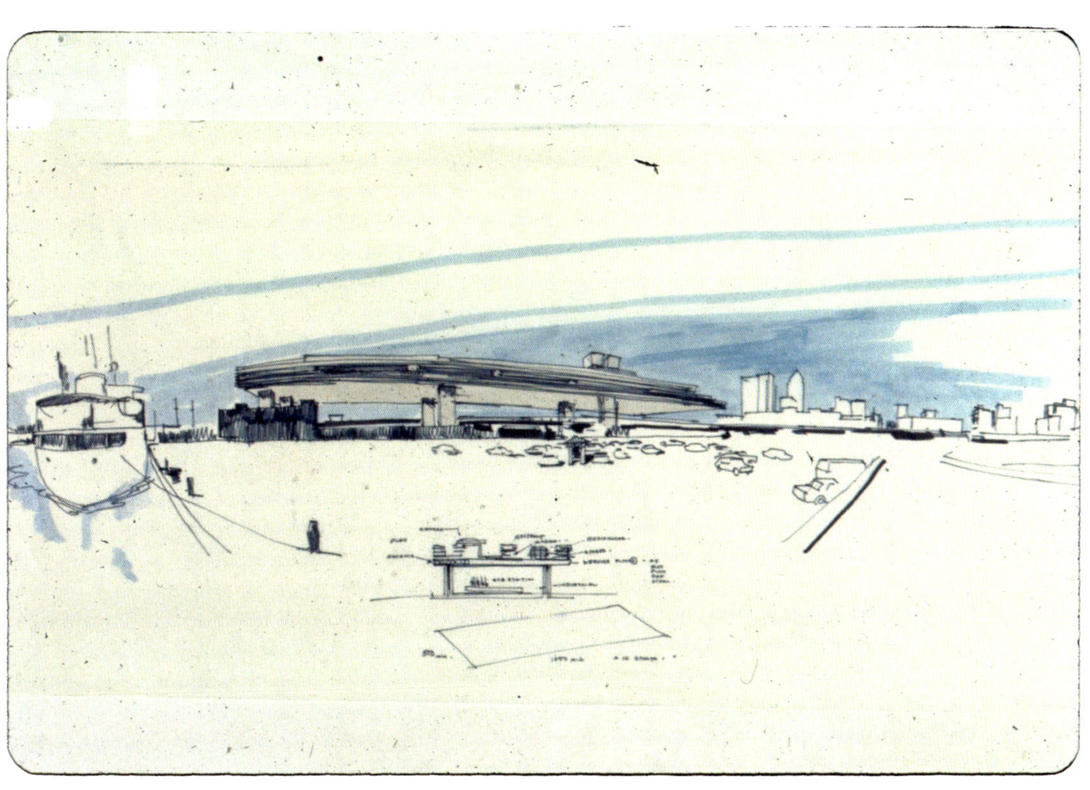

River-Urban, Miami, 1974 (unbuilt)
Master plan
Color slide
George A. Smathers Libraries, University of Florida

The Parker Plan (unbuilt)
From Nixon Smiley, "Miami at Bay," *The Miami Herald, Tropic Magazine,* January 2, 1972
Printed ephemera, 21 ½" x 13"
George A. Smathers Libraries, University of Florida

River-Urban, Miami, 1974 (unbuilt)
Perspective rendering
Color slide
George A. Smathers Libraries, University of Florida

Part V
Coda: A Life of Activity in Accordance with Reason (1973-2011)

Parker Residence (Skyview), Gainesville, 1997
Interior rendering by John G. Adams
Colored pencil on paper, 23 ¼" x 23 ¼"
George A. Smathers Libraries, University of Florida

Volcano, 1994
Watercolor, 14 ⅛" x 10 ⅛"
Courtesy of Euphrosyne Parker and Family

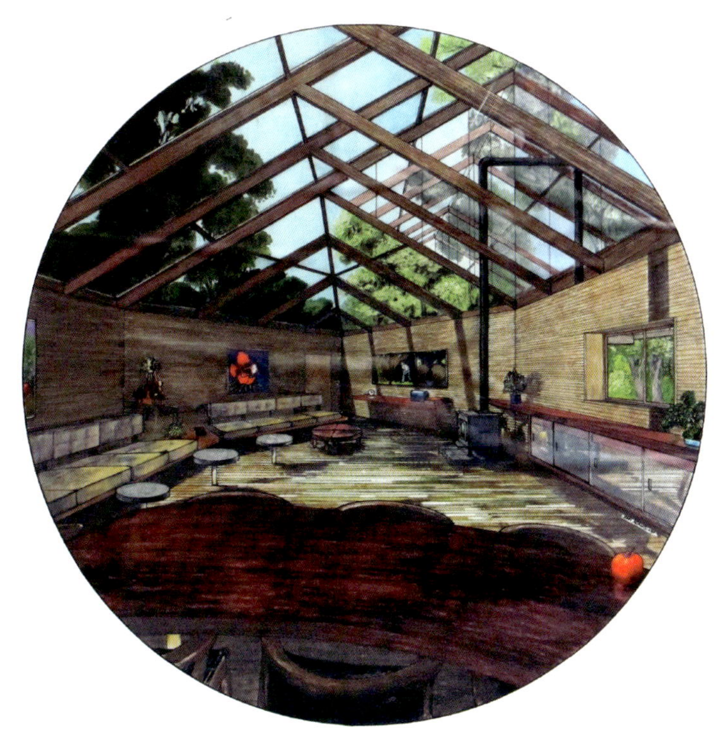

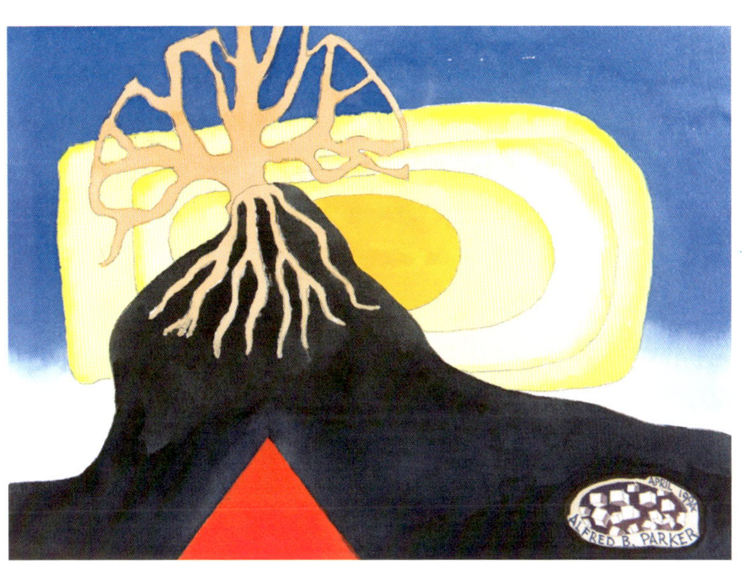
APRIL
ALFRED B. PARKER

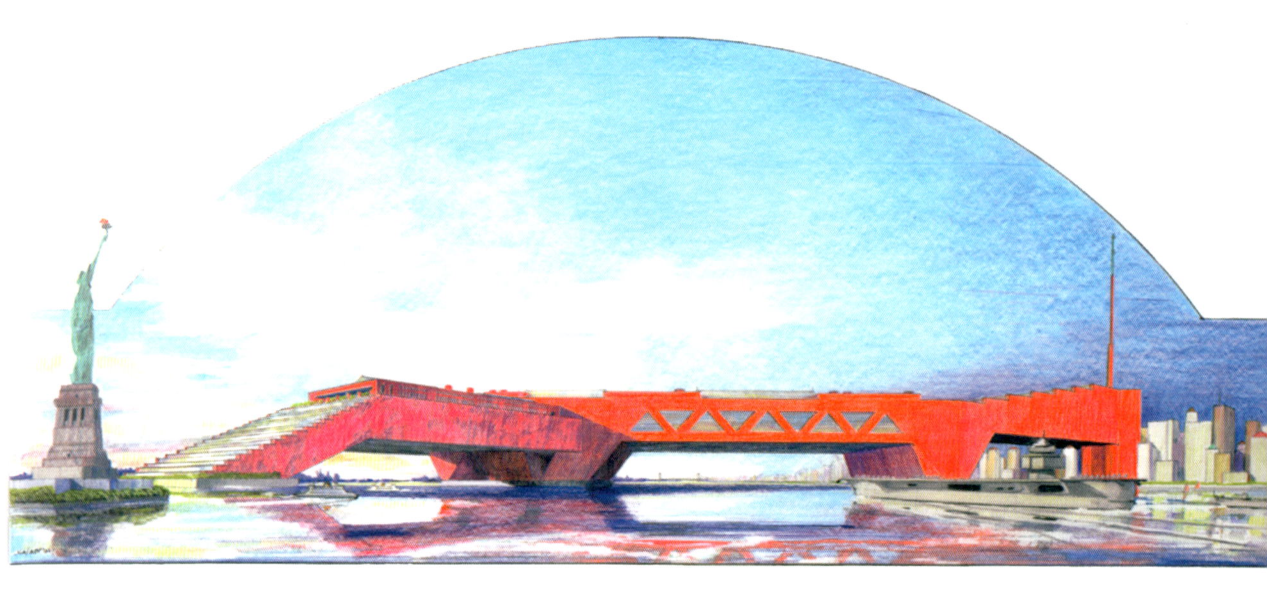

World Trade Center Project, New York City, 2001-03
Perspective rendering
Smathers Libraries, University of Florida

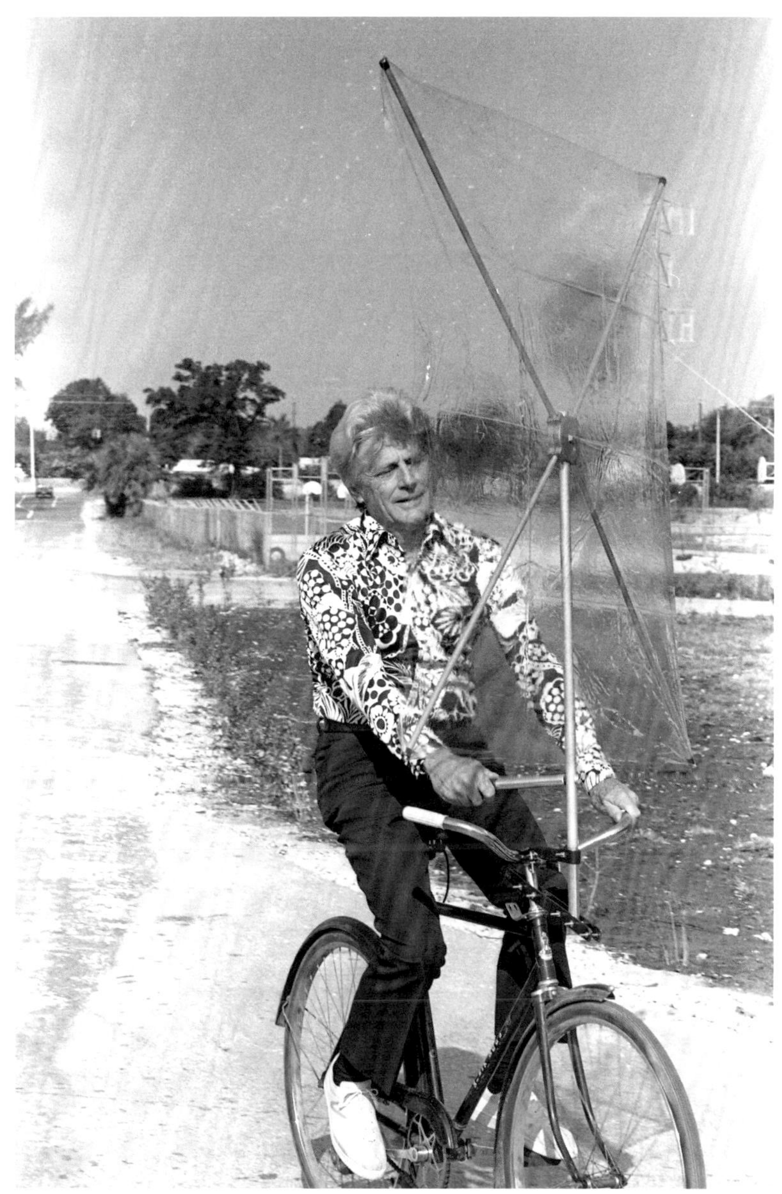

Alfred Browning Parker riding a wind-powered bicycle, December 13, 1973
B&W vintage photograph, 8" x 10"
Photograph © Tim Chapman
Tim Chapman Collection, HistoryMiami Museum

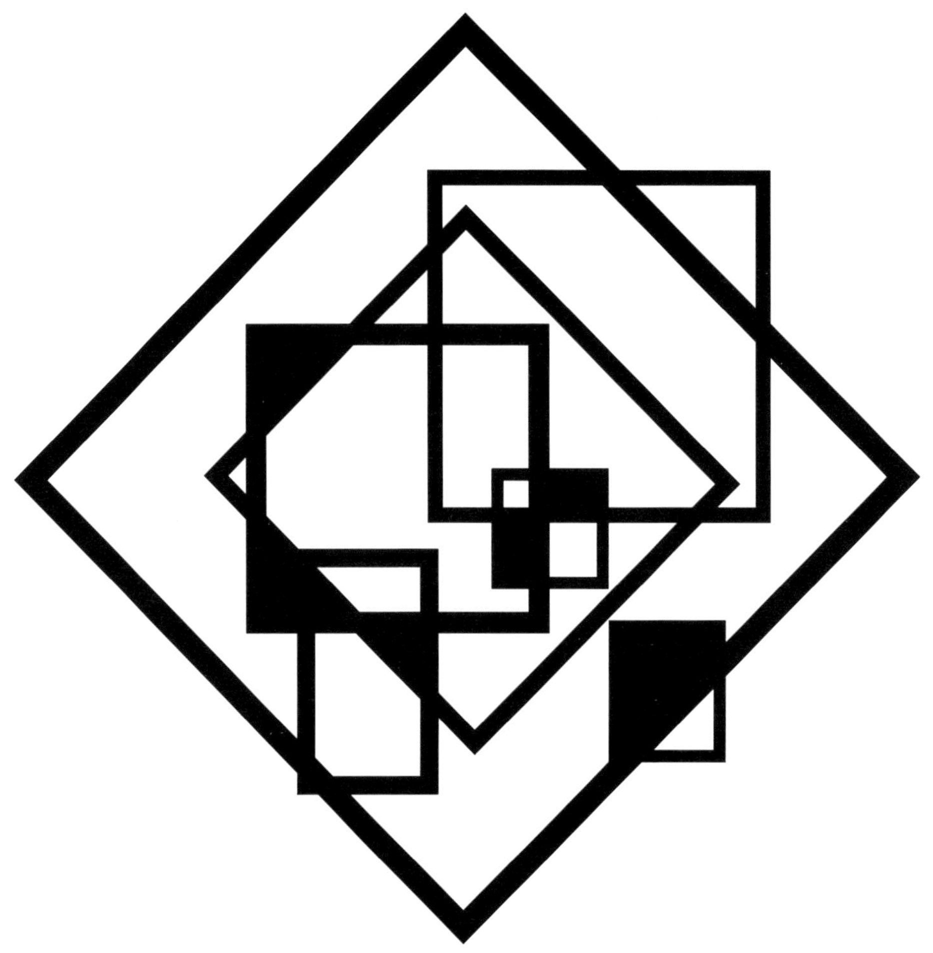

Graphic based on original fabric stamp for the Gayer Residence, Coconut Grove, 1953